A CALL TO CONSCIENCE

"A powerful presentation, a vivid portrait of an important era. More than that, King's finely honed sense of justice and morality speaks to issues of today."
—Philadelphia Inquirer

"Packed with powerful prose. . . . This book reminds readers that King wasn't simply a brilliant speaker and leader but also a brilliant thinker."
—Detroit Free Press

"What a vision! As you read . . . create another vision—this time of what we can do in the arena of public policy in the twenty-first century, a vision that brings good news to the poor, that binds up the brokenhearted, and that sets at liberty them that are bound."
—The Honorable Walter E. Fauntroy

"It was as though he had seen into the hearts and souls of people everywhere and touched their deepest longing for a shared destiny, a common purpose, a sense of mission."
—Dr. Dorothy I. Height

more . . .

A CALL TO CONSCIENCE

The LANDMARK SPEECHES of
DR. MARTIN LUTHER KING, JR.

EDITED BY CLAYBORNE CARSON
AND KRIS SHEPARD

IPM
INTELLECTUAL PROPERTIES MANAGEMENT, INC.

IN ASSOCIATION WITH

GRAND CENTRAL
PUBLISHING

NEW YORK   BOSTON

Grand Central Publishing
Hachette Book Group
237 Park Avenue
New York, NY 10017

www.HachetteBookGroup.com

Printed in the United States of America

Originally published in hardcover by Hachette Book Group.

First Trade Edition: January 2002
10 9

Grand Central Publishing is a division of Hachette Book Group, Inc.
The Grand Central Publishing name and logo is a trademark of
Hachette Book Group, Inc.

The Library of Congress has catalogd the hardcover edition as follows:

King, Martin Luther, Jr. 1929–1968.
    A call to conscience : the landmark speeches of Dr. Martin Luther
King, Jr. / edited by Clayborne Carson and Kris Shepard
        p. cm.
    ISBN 978-0-446-52399-8
    1. Afro-Americans—Civil rights. 2. Civil rights movements—United
States—History—20th cantury. 3. United States—Race relations.
I. Carson, Clayborne. 1944– II. Shepard, Kris. III. Title.

E185.97.K5 A5 2001
323'.092—dc21   00-032487

ISBN 978-0-446-67809-4 (pbk.)

Book design by Giorgetta Bell McRee
Cover design by Allison J. Warner
Cover photograph by Corbis / Bettman

CONTENTS

INTRODUCTION

BY ANDREW YOUNG

artin Luther King, Jr., was the Voice of the Century. No voice more clearly delineated the moral issues of the second half of the twentieth century and no vision more profoundly inspired people—from the American South to southern Africa, from the Berlin Wall to the Great Wall of China. Martin Luther King, Jr.'s dream of American moral possibilities expressed a universal hope for mankind that derived heavily from the Hebrew prophets, the teachings of Jesus of Nazareth, and the nonviolent actions of India's Mahatma Gandhi.

Martin's voice was more than the communication of intellectual ideals and spiritual vision. It was a call for action, action which he personally led from the early days of the Montgomery bus boycott in 1955 until his assassination in Memphis in 1968.

Martin spoke with the passion and poetry of the prophets of old. He proclaimed for our time the faith that justice can and will prevail. He saw leadership as a process of relating the daily plight of humankind to the eternal truths of creation. For him, as he proclaimed at the funeral of three of the four little girls killed in the bombing of the Sixteenth Street Baptist Church in Birmingham:

> Death is not a period that ends the great sentence of life, but a comma that punctuates it to more lofty significance. Death is not a blind alley that leads the human race into a state of nothingness, but an open door which leads man into life eternal. Let this daring faith, this great invincible surmise, be your sustaining power during these trying days.

Martin was first of all a man of faith, a preacher of the Gospel of Jesus with its hope in a resurrection not only of his spiritual body, but also the social expansion of the ideals by which he preached and lived.

Martin's life was an effort to infuse our complex political and social existence with the spiritual power of "ultimate reality," to use Paul Tillich's phrase. To the millions who were moved to rise up on the powerful emotional cadences of his oratory, it was nothing less than the voice of God coming through the life of one of his young, humble, and obedient servants. His oratory sought to forge a new state of justice with mercy through the power of truth without violence—truth that sought to bring all men and women together as brothers and sisters: truth spoken in love and mercy that believed the world's conflicts could be reconciled in the power of the human spirit without resorting to violence.

Martin never reached the age of forty, being shot by a single rifle bullet just a few months after his thirty-ninth birthday. He always knew that martyrdom was the potential price of challenging America's version of racial separation.

Try though he might, he could not escape the burden of leadership. In 1954 King left Boston University for the sleepy southern town of Montgomery, Alabama, seeking the peace and quiet of small town life. While pastor of the relatively small but prominent Dexter Avenue Baptist Church, he hoped to have the time and freedom to complete his doctoral dissertation in systematic theology. Just a few months after his dissertation was submitted, however, Rosa Parks's arrest on one of Montgomery's segregated buses and the subsequent boycott thrust him onto the national stage. He soon found himself selected *Time* magazine's Man of the Year, an honor bestowed before he was even thirty years old.

From that moment on, Martin came to symbolize and vocalize the hopes and aspirations of oppressed people all over the planet. The rich Negro spiritual "We Shall Overcome" became the nonviolent anthem of men and women the world over.

The most remarkable aspect of this moral crusade was that he expanded on Gandhi's use of nonviolence and the force of truth to liberate not only the former sons and daughters of slaves but the sons and daughters of slave owners as well. The message, though essentially spiritual, was nevertheless powerfully political, causing governments to fall, wars to end, and the courts and Congress of the United States to radically expand the human rights vision of the U.S. Constitution to include the enforcement of new freedoms for the sons and daughters of former African slaves. This same message soon inspired movements for the liberation of women, Hispanic Americans, native Americans, children, and the physically handicapped, and led, ultimately, to a "rising tide of expectations through the globe." Today's New South and the election of three sons of the South to the United States presidency can all be attributed to the struggle that Martin led to fulfill the American Dream without resorting to the destruction of either persons or property.

For Martin, social justice would not "roll in on the wings of inevitability" but would come through struggle and sacrifice.

His Montgomery speeches helped desegregate city buses. His Birmingham and Lincoln Memorial speeches sparked the passage of the Civil Rights Act of 1964, putting an end to legal segregation of the races. In Selma, he successfully called for the right to vote. His condemnation of the war in Vietnam was instrumental in ending America's involvement in that conflict. In 1968 he was killed while struggling with Memphis sanitation workers to put an end to their poverty.

This is a unique way to read and understand history: from its primary sources. These speeches grew out of and helped to shape the moral challenges of the second half of the twentieth century. This marvelous compilation of Martin's words and witness were each tied to a specific challenge of injustice. He never sought a confrontation with evil. He was essentially a husband, father, and pastor of the Baptist Church, as were his father and grandfather before him.

Events in the American South and southern Africa, as well as the relatively peaceful democratic transformation of eastern Europe, have proved him right in seeing nonviolence as the best way to resolve the world's problems, while conflicts from Bosnia to Liberia continue to prove the futility of violence.

Perhaps reading these eloquent proclamations of a man of "organized, aggressive, and positive goodwill," who loved his adversaries as brothers and who gave his life in an attempt to "redeem the soul of America from the triple evils of racism, war and poverty," will show us the way into the new millennium and help us to continue to live these truths in the days to come.

ANDREW YOUNG worked closely with Dr. King in the Southern Christian Leadership Conference on efforts such as citizenship education and voter registration. Elected to the United States House of Representatives in 1973, Young was the first black representative from Georgia since Reconstruction. After serving as U.S. ambassador to the United Nations, he was twice elected mayor of Atlanta, Georgia, and received the Presidential Medal of Freedom, America's highest civilian award. He is currently head of Good Works International, LLC.

A CALL TO
CONSCIENCE

ADDRESS TO THE FIRST MONTGOMERY IMPROVEMENT ASSOCIATION (MIA) MASS MEETING

INTRODUCTION BY ROSA LOUISE PARKS

 ecember 5, 1955, was one of the memorable and inspiring days of my life. History records this day as the beginning of the modern Civil Rights Movement that transformed America and influenced freedom revolutions around the world.

I had been arrested four days earlier, on December 1, in my hometown of Montgomery, Alabama, for refusing to get up and give my seat on a city bus to a white man, which was a much-resented customary practice at the time. Local black community leaders, the Reverend E. D. Nixon and attorney Fred Gray, asked me if I would be willing to make a test case out of my arrest, with the goal of ending segregation on Montgomery's buses, and I agreed to cooperate with them.

Mrs. Joanne Robinson and other local black women leaders of the Women's Political Council of our community met on the evening of my arrest and decided to call a boycott to begin on December 5, the day of my trial. I was found guilty of violating a segregation statute and given a suspended sentence, with a ten-dollar fine plus four dollars in court costs. This was in keeping with our legal strategy, so we could appeal and challenge the segregation law in a higher court.

A group of ministers met later in the afternoon of December 5 and formed a new organization, the Montgomery Improvement Association. An open meeting of the black community was called for that evening at the Holt Street Baptist Church. The ministers elected a young minister named Martin Luther King, Jr., whom I had met briefly a few months before, to serve as its first president and spokesman. Dr. King was chosen in part because he was relatively new to the community and so did not have any enemies. Also Dr. King had made a strong impression on Rufus Lewis, an influential member of our community who attended Dr. King's Dexter Avenue Baptist Church. I had met Dr. King's wife, Coretta, and had attended concerts where she sang, but I didn't know she was his wife at the time.

By the time I arrived at the meeting, the church was so filled up that a crowd of hundreds spilled out into the street, and speakers had to be set up outside to accommodate everyone. The excitement around the church was electrifying, and I remember having a sense that something powerful was being born. I squeezed my way through the crowd to my seat on the platform, where a lively discussion about the boycott strategy was underway.

Then Dr. King was introduced to the audience and began to speak in the rich, poised baritone and learned eloquence that distinguished even this debut speech of his career as a civil rights leader. Later Dr. King would write that he normally took fifteen hours to prepare his sermons, but because of the hectic events of the day, he'd had only twenty minutes to prepare for "the most decisive speech of my life." He spent five minutes of his time worrying about it, and then wisely prayed to God for guidance.

His prayer must have been heard, because on that historic night, despite all of the pressure on him, Dr. King showed no trace of doubt or hesitancy. He spoke like a seasoned preacher and was frequently interrupted throughout his remarks by an energetic chorus of "Amen," "That's right," "Keep talkin'," and "Yes, Lord."

Dr. King recounted the abuses Montgomery's black citizens had experienced leading up to the boycott. He spoke about what had happened to me and why we must win this struggle. He told the crowd that our boycott was a patriotic protest, very much in the tradition of American democracy. He underscored the critical importance of honoring the principles of nonviolence and rooting our protest in the teachings of Jesus Christ, alongside our unshakable determination to win the boycott.

And then, as he concluded, he said the words that I will never forget, the prophetic words that, for me, still define the character of our nonviolent freedom movement: "When the history books are written in the future, somebody will have to say, 'There lived a race of people, a black people, fleecy locks and black complexion, a people who had the moral courage to stand up for their rights. And thereby they injected a new meaning into the veins of history and of civilization.'"

Amid the thundering applause that met the conclusion of Dr. King's speech on that night, there was a sense that this speech had launched a brave new era. Dr. King had spelled it out with clarity and eloquence: This movement was not just about desegregating the buses, or even just the mistreatment of our people in Montgomery. This movement was about slaking the centuries-old thirst of a long-suffering people for freedom, dignity, and human rights. It was time to drink at the well.

In these pages we celebrate the wonderful oratory of one of America's greatest leaders. But let us remember that what gave his speeches and sermons legitimacy was that Dr. King didn't just talk the talk; he walked the walk from Montgomery to Memphis, enduring jails, beatings, abuse, threats, the bombing of his home, and the highest sacrifice a person can make for a righteous cause.

When I entered the courtroom that morning, I heard one of our supporters chanting, "They messed with the wrong one now." But when I headed home after Dr. King's speech I knew that we had found the right one to articulate our protest. As the weeks and months wore on, it became clear to me that we had found our Moses, and he would surely lead us to the promised land of liberty and justice for all.

ROSA LOUISE PARKS was a civil rights activist and local NAACP official in Montgomery, Alabama, for over a decade before her refusal to abide by segregated bus-seating practices on December 1, 1955, sparked the successful Montgomery bus boycott. Parks, facing the loss of her job and other forms of intimidation, left Montgomery for Detroit, Michigan, where she continued her political work and cofounded the Rosa and Raymond Parks Institute for Self Development.

ADDRESS TO THE FIRST MONTGOMERY IMPROVEMENT ASSOCIATION (MIA) MASS MEETING

My friends, we are certainly very happy to see each of you out this evening. We are here this evening for serious business. [*Audience:*] (*Yes*) We are here in a general sense because first and foremost we are American citizens (*That's right*) and we are determined to apply our citizenship to the fullness of its meaning. (*Yeah, That's right*) We are here also because of our love for democracy (*Yes*), because of our deep-seated belief that democracy transformed from thin paper to thick action (*Yes*) is the greatest form of government on earth. (*That's right*)

But we are here in a specific sense because of the bus situation in Montgomery. (*Yes*) We are here because we are determined to get the situation corrected. This situation is not at all new. The problem has existed over endless years. (*That's right*) For many years now, Negroes in Montgomery and so many other areas have been inflicted with the paralysis of crippling fear (*Yes*) on buses in our community. (*That's right*) On so many occasions, Negroes have been intimidated and humiliated and impressed—oppressed—because of the sheer fact that they were Negroes. (*That's right*)

I don't have time this evening to go into the history of these numerous cases. Many of them now are lost in the thick fog of oblivion (*Yes*), but at least one stands before us now with glaring dimensions. (*Yes*)

Just the other day, just last Thursday to be exact, one of the finest citizens in Montgomery (*Amen*)—not one of the finest Negro citizens (*That's right*), but one of the finest citizens in Montgomery—was taken from a bus (*Yes*) and carried to jail and arrested (*Yes*) because she refused to get up to give her seat to a white person. (*Yes, That's right*) Now the press would have us believe that she refused to leave a reserved section for Negroes (*Yes*), but I want you to know this evening that there is no reserved section. (*All right*) The law has never been clarified at that point. (*Hell no*) Now I think I speak with, with legal authority—not that I have any legal authority, but I think I speak with legal authority behind me (*All right*)—that the law, the ordinance, the city ordinance has never been totally clarified. (*That's right*)

Mrs. Rosa Parks is a fine person. (*Well, Well said*) And, since it had to happen, I'm happy that it happened to a person like Mrs. Parks (*Yes*), for nobody can doubt the boundless outreach of her integrity. (*Sure enough*) Nobody can doubt the height of her character (*Yes*), nobody can doubt the depth of her Christian commitment and devotion to the teachings of Jesus. (*All right*) And I'm happy, since it had to happen, it happened to a person that nobody can call a disturbing factor in the community. (*All right*) Mrs. Parks is a fine Christian person, unassuming, and yet there is integrity and character there. And just because she refused to get up, she was arrested.

And you know, my friends, there comes a time when people get tired of being trampled over by the iron feet of oppression. [*Sustained applause*] There comes a time, my friends, when people get tired of being plunged across the abyss of humiliation, where they experience the bleakness of nagging despair. (*Keep talking*) There comes a time when people get tired of being pushed out of the glittering sunlight of life's July and left standing amid the piercing chill of an alpine November. (*That's right*) [*Applause*] There comes a time. (*Yes sir, Teach*) [*Applause continues*]

We are here, we are here this evening because we are tired now. (*Yes*) [*Applause*] And I want to say that we are not here advocating violence. (*No*) We have never done that. (*Repeat that, Repeat that*) [*Applause*] I want it to be known throughout Montgomery and throughout this nation (*Well*) that we are Christian people. (*Yes*) [*Applause*] We believe in the Christian religion. We believe in the teachings of Jesus. (*Well*) The only weapon that we have in our hands this evening is the weapon of protest. (*Yes*) [*Applause*] That's all.

And certainly, certainly, this is the glory of America, with all of its faults. (*Yeah*) This is the glory of our democracy. If we were incarcerated behind the iron curtains of a Communistic nation we couldn't do this. If we were dropped in the dungeon of a totalitarian regime we couldn't do this. (*All right*) But the great glory of American democracy is the right to protest for right. (*That's right*) [*Applause*] My friends, don't let anybody make us feel that we are to be compared in our actions with the Ku Klux Klan or with the White Citizens' Council. [*Applause*] There will be no crosses burned at any bus stops in Montgomery. (*Well, That's right*) There will be no white persons pulled out of their homes and taken out on some distant road and lynched for not cooperating. [*Applause*] There will be nobody amid, among us who will stand up and defy the Constitution of this nation. [*Applause*] We only assemble here because of our desire to see right exist. [*Applause*] My friends, I want it to be known that we're going to work with grim and bold determination to gain justice on the buses in this city. [*Applause*]

And we are not wrong, we are not wrong in what we are doing. (*Well*) If we are wrong, the Supreme Court of this nation is wrong. (*Yes sir*) [*Applause*] If we are wrong, the Constitution of the United States is wrong. (*Yes*) [*Applause*] If we are wrong, God Almighty is wrong. (*That's right*) [*Applause*] If we are wrong, Jesus of Nazareth was merely a utopian dreamer that never came down to earth. (*Yes*) [*Applause*] If we are wrong, justice is a lie. (*Yes*) Love has no meaning. [*Applause*] And we are determined here in Montgomery to work and fight until justice runs down like water (*Yes*) [*Applause*], and righteousness like a mighty stream. (*Keep talking*) [*Applause*]

I want to say that in all of our actions, we must stick together. (*That's right*) [*Applause*] Unity is the great need of the hour (*Well, That's right*), and if we are united we can get many of the things that we not only desire but which we justly deserve. (*Yeah*) And don't let anybody frighten you. (*Yeah*) We are not afraid of what we are doing (*Oh no*), because we are doing it within the law. (*All right*) There is never a time in our American democracy that we must ever think we are wrong when we protest. (*Yes sir*) We reserve that right. When labor all over this nation came to see that it would be trampled over by capitalistic power, it was nothing wrong with labor getting together and organizing and protesting for its rights. (*That's right*)

We, the disinherited of this land, we who have been oppressed so long, are tired of going through the long night of captivity. And now we are reaching out for the daybreak of freedom and justice and equality. [*Applause*] May I say to you, my friends, as I come to a close, and just giving some idea of why we are assembled here, that we must keep—and I want to stress this, in all of our doings, in all of our deliberations here this evening and all of the week and while—whatever we do, we must keep God in the forefront. (*Yeah*) Let us be Christian in all of our actions. (*That's right*) But I want to tell you this evening that it is not enough for us to talk about love, love is one of the pivotal points of the Christian faith. There is another side called justice. And justice is really love in calculation. (*All right*) Justice is love correcting that which revolts against love. (*Well*)

The Almighty God himself is not the only, not the God just standing out saying through Hosea, "I love you, Israel." He's also the God that stands up before the nations and said: "Be still and know that I'm God (*Yeah*), that if you don't obey me I will break the

‡ 11 ‡

backbone of your power (*Yeah*) and slap you out of the orbits of your international and national relationships." (*That's right*) Standing beside love is always justice, and we are only using the tools of justice. Not only are we using the tools of persuasion, but we've come to see that we've got to use the tools of coercion. Not only is this thing a process of education, but it is also a process of legislation. [*Applause*]

And as we stand and sit here this evening and as we prepare ourselves for what lies ahead, let us go out with the grim and bold determination that we are going to stick together. [*Applause*] We are going to work together. [*Applause*] Right here in Montgomery, when the history books are written in the future (*Yes*), somebody will have to say, "There lived a race of people (*Well*), a *black* people (*Yes sir*), fleecy locks and black complexion (*Yes*), a people who had the moral courage to stand up for their rights. [*Applause*] And thereby they injected a new meaning into the veins of history and of civilization." And we're going to do that. God grant that we will do it before it is too late. (*Oh yeah*) As we proceed with our program, let us think of these things. (*Yes*) [*Applause*]

━┥━•━┝━

DELIVERED AT HOLT STREET BAPTIST CHURCH,
MONTGOMERY, ALABAMA,
5 DECEMBER 1955.

THE BIRTH
OF A
NEW NATION

INTRODUCTION BY REVEREND LEON H. SULLIVAN

uring his last speech delivered in Memphis, Tennessee, prior to his assassination, Martin Luther King said, "I've been to the mountaintop.... And I've looked over, and I've seen the Promised Land." Dr. King is still on the mountaintop looking down on us, guiding our steps in human rights, justice, and nonviolence as we try to get to the Promised Land.

The speech that follows, titled "The Birth of a New Nation," was preached at the Dexter Avenue Baptist Church in Montgomery, Alabama, April 7, 1957. In this sermon Dr. King dealt with the independence of Ghana from the domination and oppression of the British Empire, tying the liberation of Ghana to the liberation and freedom needs for people in America and the world—and setting the stage for all of God's children around the world seeking justice and equal opportunity for themselves, their children, and their children's children. Detailing the exodus of the Jews out of Egypt under the leadership of Moses, Dr. King's sermon tells the story of how God moves in the events of time and describes the success of peoples struggling for freedom and justice with determination, faith, nonviolence, and reliance on the strength and power of God.

"The Birth of a New Nation" is a chronicle of these efforts led by a man of faith in the old African Gold Coast, Kwame Nkrumah, born of illiterate parents and with little but his own determination and the help of God to assist him in his impossible dream: to give birth to a new nation, free from the colonization of the British Empire. A young man born of destiny rose above the impossible to help free a nation and become the leader of his country.

At the time this sermon was delivered, Dr. King was perhaps the only man alive who, through his own experience, could put the history of oppression into a tangible context. Dr. King lived through the kind of times Moses, Gandhi, and Nkrumah faced in their day, meeting impossible odds and overcoming them for the liberation of their peoples. "The Birth of a New Nation," Dr. King said, "is something of the story of every people struggling for freedom. . . . And it demonstrates the stages that seem to inevitably follow the quest for freedom."

Dr. King tells of the inspiring and riveting Kwame Nkrumah, who worked in Philadelphia as a bellhop and dishwasher as he struggled through school. He returned home, spent years in prison for his activism, was finally freed . . . and elected the first prime minister of Ghana. Walking into the ceremonies with all of his ministers "with prison caps and the coats that they had lived with for all of the months that they had been in prison," Nkrumah stood up and made his closing speech to Parliament formalizing the birth of a nation. Said Dr. King in his sermon, "That was a great hour. An old Parliament passing away . . . a new nation being born."

Being there that day with other leaders from America, including Ralph Bunche, King's wonderful wife Coretta (who following his assassination continued the present-day vigil of nonviolence in America), and Congressman Charles Diggs, I witnessed the tale of the impossible becoming true. It was the breaking loose from Egypt: "We could hear it from every corner, ever nook and crook of the community: 'Freedom! Freedom!'" Watching the new leader of Ghana waltz with the duchess of Kent, representing the queen of England, was as revolutionary as it was wonderful.

Dr. King, already leading a life similar to that of Moses, Gandhi, and Nkrumah, was about to take the next step of these brilliant leaders: entering the wilderness to forge a new America for blacks and for whites, achieving the equality and justice denied since the days of slavery. What a message for young people to read and know! Faith, determination, and help from God can do such great things.

Dr. King's dreams for the coming of an emerging independent Africa connect directly with the involvement and assistance of black people from America and throughout the world. Because of his deep concern for the future of Africa, I have no doubt but

that had Dr. King lived, he would have linked those
dreams with the realization of a new Africa and initiated the pilgrimages to Africa like the African–
African-American Summits since 1991 (all of which
have been attended by Coretta King) . . . and I would
have been a proud follower of Dr. King, as he led
these pilgrimages for a new birth of a new promised
land.

LEON H. SULLIVAN, former pastor of the influential Zion Baptist Church in Philadelphia, initiated a selective boycott of
Philadelphia employers who refused to hire black workers in
the late 1950s. In 1964 he founded the Opportunities Industrialization Center, which provides skills training throughout the United States and Africa. Sullivan was actively involved
in the divestiture movement against South Africa's apartheid
government and was awarded the Presidential Medal of Freedom in 1992.

The Birth
of a
New Nation

I want to preach this morning from the subject: "The Birth of a New Nation." And I would like to use as a basis for our thinking together, a story that has long since been stenciled on the mental sheets of succeeding generations. It is the story of the Exodus, the story of the flight of the Hebrew people from the bondage of Egypt, through the wilderness, and finally to the Promised Land. It's a beautiful story. I had the privilege the other night of seeing the story in movie terms in New York City, entitled *The Ten Commandments*, and I came to see it in all of its beauty. The struggle of Moses, the struggle of his devoted followers as they sought to get out of Egypt. And they finally moved on to the wilderness and toward the Promised Land. This is something of the story of every people struggling for freedom. It is the first story of man's explicit quest for freedom. And it demonstrates the stages that seem to inevitably follow the quest for freedom.

Prior to March the sixth, 1957, there existed a country known as the Gold Coast. This country was a colony of the British Empire. This country was situated in that vast continent known as Africa. I'm sure you know a great deal about Africa, that continent with some two hundred million people, and it extends and covers a great deal of territory. There are many familiar names associated with Africa that you would probably remember, and there are some countries in Africa that many people never realize. For instance, Egypt is in Africa. And there is that vast area of North Africa with Egypt and Ethiopia, with Tunisia and Algeria and Morocco and Libya. Then you might move to South Africa and you think of that extensive territory known as the Union of South Africa. There is that capital city Johannesburg that you read so much about these days. Then there is central Africa with places like Rhodesia and the Belgian Congo. And then there is East Africa with places like Kenya and Tanganyika, and places like Uganda and other very powerful countries right there. And then you move over to West Africa, where you find the French West Africa and Nigeria, and Liberia and Sierra Leone and places like that. And it is in this spot, in this section of Africa, that we find the Gold Coast, there in West Africa.

You also know that for years and for centuries, Africa has been one of the most exploited continents in the history of the world. It's been the "Dark Continent." It's been the continent that has suffered all of the pain and the affliction that could be mustered up by other nations. And it is that continent which has experienced slavery, which has experienced all of the lowest standards that we can think about, and it's been brought into being by the exploitation inflicted upon it by other nations.

And this country, the Gold Coast, was a part of this extensive continent known as Africa. It's a little country there in West Africa about ninety-one thousand miles in area, with a population of about five million people, a little more than four and a half million. And it stands there with its capital city, Accra. For years the Gold Coast was exploited and dominated and trampled over. The first European settlers came in there about 1444, the Portuguese, and they started legitimate trade with the people in the Gold Coast. They started dealing with them with their gold, and in turn they gave them guns and ammunition and gunpowder and that type of thing. Well, pretty soon America was discovered a few years later in the fourteen hundreds, and then the British West Indies. And all of these growing discoveries brought about the slave trade.

You remember it started in America in 1619. And there was a big scramble for power in Africa. With the growth of the slave trade, there came into Africa, into the Gold Coast in particular, not only the Portuguese but also the Swedes and the Danes and the Dutch and the British. And all of these nations competed with each other to win the power of the Gold Coast so that they could exploit these people for commercial reasons and sell them into slavery.

Finally, in 1850, Britain won out, and she gained possession of the total territorial expansion of the Gold Coast. From 1850 to 1957, March sixth, the Gold Coast was a colony of the British Empire. And as a colony she suffered all of the injustices, all of the exploitation, all of the humiliation that comes as a result of colonialism. But like all slavery, like all domination, like all exploitation, it came to the point that the people got tired of it.

And that seems to be the long story of history. There seems to be a throbbing desire, there seems to be an internal desire for freedom within the soul of every man. And it's there: it might not break forth in the beginning, but eventually it breaks out. Men realize that, that freedom is something basic. To rob a man of his freedom is to take from him the essential basis of his manhood. To take from him his freedom is to rob him of something of God's image. To paraphrase the words of Shakespeare's *Othello*: "Who steals my purse steals trash; 'tis something, nothing; 'twas mine, 'tis his, has been the slave of thousands; But he who filches from me my freedom robs me of that which not enriches him, but makes me poor indeed."

There is something in the soul that cries out for freedom. There is something deep down within the very soul of man that reaches out for Canaan. Men cannot be satisfied with Egypt. They tried to adjust to it for a while. Many men have vested interests in Egypt, and they are slow to leave. Egypt makes it profitable to them, some people profit by Egypt. The vast majority, the masses of people never profit by Egypt, and they are never content with it. And eventually they rise up and begin to cry out for Canaan's land.

And so these people got tired. It had a long history. As far back as 1844, the chiefs themselves of the Gold Coast rose up and came together and revolted against the British Empire and the other powers that were in existence at that time dominating the Gold Coast. They revolted, saying that they wanted to govern themselves. But these powers clamped down on them, and the British said that we will not let you go.

About 1909, a young man was born on the twelfth of September. History didn't know at that time what that young man had in his mind. His mother and father, illiterate, not a part of the powerful tribal life of Africa, not chiefs at all, but humble people. And that boy grew up, he went to school at Achimota for a while in Africa, and then he finished there with honors and decided to work his way to America. And he landed to America one day with about fifty dollars in his pocket in terms of pounds, getting ready to get an education. And he went down to Pennsylvania, to Lincoln University. He started studying there, and he started reading the great insights of the philosophers, he started reading the great insights of the ages. And he finished there and took his theological degree there and preached awhile around Philadelphia and other areas as he was in the country. And went over to the University of Pennsylvania and took up a master's there in philosophy and sociology. All the years that he stood in America, he was poor, he had to work hard. He says in his autobiography how he worked as a bellhop in hotels, as a dishwasher, and during the summer how he worked as a waiter trying to struggle through school. [*Recording interrupted*]

"I want to go back home. I want to go back to West Africa, the land of my people, my native land.

There is some work to be done there." He got a ship and went to London and stopped for a while by London School of Economy and picked up another degree there. Then while in London, he came, he started thinking about Pan-Africanism, and the problem of how to free his people from colonialism. For as he said, he always realized that colonialism was made for domination and for exploitation. It was made to keep a certain group down and exploit that group economically for the advantage of another. He studied and thought about all of this, and one day he decided to go back to Africa.

He got to Africa and he was immediately elected the executive secretary of the United Party of the Gold Coast. And he worked hard, and he started getting a following. And the people in this party, the old, the people who had had their hands on the plow for a long time, thought he was pushing a little too fast, and they got a little jealous of his influence. And so finally he had to break from the United Party of the Gold Coast, and in 1949 he organized the Convention People's Party. It was this party that started out working for the independence of the Gold Coast. He started out in a humble way, urging his people to unite for freedom. And urging the officials of the British Empire to give them freedom. They were slow to respond, but the masses of people were with him, and they had united to become the most powerful and influential party that had ever been organized in that section of Africa.

He started writing, and his companions with him and many of them started writing so much that the officials got afraid, and they put them in jail, and Nkrumah himself was finally placed in jail for several years because he was a seditious man. He was an agitator. He was imprisoned on the basis of sedition. And he was placed there to stay in prison for many years, but he had inspired some people outside of prison. They got together just a few months after he'd been in prison and elected him the prime minister while he was in prison. For a while the British officials tried to keep him there, and Gbedemah says—one of his close associates, the minister of finance, Mr. Gbedemah—said that that night the people were getting ready to go down to the jail and get him out, but Gbedemah said, "This isn't the way, we can't do it like this, violence will break out and we will defeat our purpose." But the British Empire saw that they had better let him out. And in a few hours Kwame Nkrumah was out of jail, the prime minister of the Gold Coast. He was placed there for fifteen years but he only served eight or nine months. And now he comes out, the prime minister of the Gold Coast.

And this was the struggling that had been going on for years. It was now coming to the point that this little nation was moving toward its independence. Then came the continual agitation, the continual resistance, so that the British Empire saw that it could no longer rule the Gold Coast. And they agreed that on the sixth of March, 1957, they would release this nation, that this nation would no longer be a colony of the British Empire, that this nation would be a sovereign nation within the British Commonwealth. All of this was because of the persistent protest, the continual agitation on the part of Prime Minister Kwame Nkrumah and the other leaders who worked along with him and the masses of people who were willing to follow.

So that day finally came. It was a great day. The week ahead was a great week. They had been preparing for this day for many years, and now it was here. People coming in from all over the world. They had started getting in by the second of March. Seventy nations represented to come to say to this new nation: "We greet you. And we give you our moral support. We hope for you God's guidance as you move now into the realm of independence." From America, itself, more than a hundred persons: the press, the diplomatic guests, and the prime minister's guests. And oh, it was a beautiful experience to see some of the leading persons on the scene of civil rights in America on hand to say, "Greetings to you," as this new nation was born. Look over, to my right is Adam Powell, to my left is Charles Diggs, to my right again is Ralph Bunche. To the other side is Her Majesty's first minister of Jamaica, Manning, Ambassador Jones of Liberia. All of these people from America, Mordecai Johnson, Horace Mann Bond, all of these people just going over to say, "We want to greet you and we want you to know that you have our moral support as you grow." Then you look out and see the vice president of the United States, you see A. Philip Randolph, you see all of the people who have stood in the forefront of the struggle for civil rights over the years, coming over to Africa to say we bid you godspeed. This was a great day not only for Nkrumah, but for the whole of the Gold Coast. There, then came Tuesday, [*March*] the fifth, many events leading up to it. That night, we walked into the closing of Parliament. The closing of the old Parliament. The old Parliament, which was, which presided over by the British Empire. The old Parliament which designated colonialism and imperialism. Now that Parliament is closing. That was a great sight and a great picture and a great scene. We sat there that night, just about five hundred able to get in there. People, thousands and thousands of people waiting outside, just about five hundred in there, and we were fortunate enough to be sitting there at that moment as guests of the prime minister. At that hour we noticed Prime Minister Nkrumah walking in, with all of his ministers, with his justices of the Supreme Court of the Gold Coast, and with all of the people of the Convention People's Party, the leaders of that party. Nkrumah came up to make his closing speech to the old Gold Coast. There was something old now passing away.

The thing that impressed me more than anything else that night was the fact that when Nkrumah walked in, and his other ministers who had been in prison with him, they didn't come in with the crowns and all of the garments of kings, but they walked in with prison caps and the coats that they had lived with for all of the months that they had been in prison. Nkrumah stood up and made his closing speech to Parliament with the little cap that he wore in prison for several months and the coat that he wore in prison for several months, and all of his ministers round about him. That was a great hour. An old Parliament passing away. And then at twelve o'clock that night we walked out. As we walked out, we noticed all over the polo grounds almost a half a million people. They had waited for this hour and this moment for years.

As we walked out of the door and looked at that beautiful building, we looked up to the top of it. And there was a little flag that had been flowing around the sky for many years. It was the Union Jack flag of the Gold Coast, the British flag, you see. But at twelve o'clock that night we saw a little flag coming down and another flag went up. The old Union Jack flag came down and the new flag of Ghana went up. This was a new nation now, a new nation being born. And when Prime Minister Nkrumah stood up before his people out in the polo ground and said, "We are no longer a British colony, we are a free, sovereign people," all over that vast throng of people we could see tears. And I stood there thinking about so many things. Before I knew it, I started weeping. I was crying for joy. And I knew about all of the struggles, and all of the pain, and all of the agony that these people had gone through for this moment.

After Nkrumah had made that final speech, it was about twelve-thirty now. And we walked away. And we could hear little children six years old and old people eighty and ninety years old walking the streets of Accra crying: "Freedom! Freedom!" They couldn't say it in the sense that we'd say it, many of them don't speak English too well, but they had their accents and it could ring out "free-doom!" They were crying it in a sense that they had never heard it before. And I could hear that old Negro spiritual once more crying out: "Free at last, free at last, Great God Almighty, I'm free at last." They were experiencing that in their very souls. And everywhere we turned, we could hear it ringing out from the housetops. We could hear it from every corner, every nook and crook of the community: "Freedom! Freedom!" This was the birth of a new nation. This was the breaking aloose from Egypt.

Wednesday morning the official opening of Parliament was held. There again we were able to get on the inside. There Nkrumah made his new speech. And now the prime minister of the Gold Coast with no superior, with all of the power that Macmillan of England has, with all of the power that Nehru of India has, now a free nation, now the prime minister of a sovereign nation. Duchess of Kent walked in, the duchess of Kent, who represented the queen of England, no longer had authority now. She was just a passing visitor now. The night before she was the official leader and spokesman for the queen, thereby the power behind the throne of the Gold Coast. But now it's Ghana, it's a new nation now, and she's just an official visitor like M. L. King and Ralph Bunche and Coretta King and everybody else, because this is a new nation. A new Ghana has come into being. And now Nkrumah stands the leader of that great nation, and when he drives out, the people standing around the streets of the city after Parliament is open, cry out: "All hail, Nkrumah!" The name of Nkrumah crowning around the whole city, everybody crying this name because they knew he had suffered for them, he had sacrificed for them, he'd gone to jail for them. This was the birth of a new nation.

This nation was now out of Egypt and had crossed the Red Sea. Now it will confront its wilderness. Like any breaking aloose from Egypt, there is a wilderness ahead. There is a problem of adjustment. Nkrumah realizes that. There is always this wilderness standing before him. For instance, it's a one-crop country, cocoa mainly. Sixty percent of the cocoa of the world comes from the Gold Coast or from Ghana. In order to make the economic system more stable, it will be necessary to industrialize. Cocoa is too fluctuating to base a whole economy on that. So there is the necessity of industrializing. Nkrumah said to me that one of the first things that he will do is to work toward industrialization.

And also he plans to work toward the whole problem of increasing the cultural standards of the community. Still ninety percent of the people are illiterate, and it is necessary to lift the whole cultural standard of the community in order to make it possible to stand up in the free world. Yes, there is a wilderness ahead, though it is my hope that even people from America will go to Africa as immigrants, right there to the Gold Coast and lend their technical assistance. For there is great need and rich, there are rich opportunities there. Right now is the time that American Negroes can lend their technical assistance to a growing new nation. I was very happy to see already, people who have moved in and making good. The son of the late president of Bennett College, Dr. Jones, is there, who started an insurance company and making good, going to the top. A doctor from Brooklyn, New York, had just come in that week and his wife is also a dentist, and they are living there now, going in there and working, and the people love them. There will be hundreds and thousands of people, I'm sure, going over to make for the growth of this new nation. And Nkrumah made it very clear to me that he would welcome any persons coming there as immigrants and to live there. Now don't think that because they have five million people the nation can't grow, that that's a small nation to be overlooked. Never forget the fact that when America was born in 1776, when it received its independence from the British Empire, there were fewer, less than four million people in America, and today it's more than a hundred and sixty million. So never underestimate a people because it's small now. America was smaller than Ghana when it was born.

There is a great day ahead. The future is on its side. It's going now through the wilderness. But the Promised Land is ahead.

And I want to take just a few more minutes as I close to say three or four things that this reminds us of and things that it says to us. Things that we must never forget as we ourselves find ourselves breaking aloose from an evil Egypt, trying to move through the wilderness toward the promised land of cultural integration: Ghana has something to say to us. It says to us first, that the oppressor never voluntarily gives freedom to the oppressed. You have to work for it. And if Nkrumah and the people of the Gold Coast had not stood up persistently, revolting against the system, it would still be a colony of the British Empire. Freedom is never given to anybody. For the oppressor has you in domination because he plans to keep you there, and he never voluntarily gives it up. And that is where the strong resistance comes. Privileged classes never give up their privileges without strong resistance.

So don't go out this morning with any illusions. Don't go back into your homes and around Montgomery thinking that the Montgomery City Commission and that all of the forces in the leadership of the South will eventually work out this thing for Negroes, it's going to work out, it's going to roll in on the wheels of inevitability. If we wait for it to work itself out, it will *never* be worked out! Freedom only comes through persistent revolt, through persistent agitation, through persistently rising up against the system of evil. The bus protest is just the beginning. Buses are integrated in Montgomery, but that is just the beginning. And don't sit down and do nothing now because the buses are integrated, because, if you stop now, we will be in the dungeons of segregation and discrimination for another hundred years. And our children and our children's children will suffer all of the bondage that we have lived under for years. It never comes voluntarily. We've got to keep on keeping on in order to gain freedom. It never comes like that. It would be fortunate if the people in power had sense enough to go on and give up, but they don't do it like that. It is not done voluntarily, but it is done through the pressure that comes about from people who are oppressed.

If there had not been a Gandhi in India with all of his noble followers, India would have never been free. If there had not been an Nkrumah and his followers in Ghana, Ghana would still be a British colony. If there had not been abolitionists in America, both Negro and white, we might still stand today in the dungeons of slavery. And then because there have been, in every period, there are always those people in every period of human history who don't mind getting their necks cut off, who don't mind being persecuted and discriminated and kicked about, because they know that freedom is never given out, but it comes through the persistent and the continual agitation and revolt on the part of those who are caught in the system. Ghana teaches us that.

It says to us another thing. It reminds us of the fact that a nation or a people can break aloose from oppression without violence. Nkrumah says in the first two pages of his autobiography, which was published on the sixth of March—a great book which you ought to read—he said that he had studied the social systems of social philosophers and he started studying the life of Gandhi and his techniques. And he said that in the beginning he could not see how they could ever get aloose from colonialism without armed revolt, without armies and ammunition, rising up. Then he says after he continued to study Gandhi and continued to study this technique, he came to see that the only way was through nonviolent positive action. And he called his program "positive action." And it's a beautiful thing, isn't it? That here is a nation that is now free, and it is free without rising up with arms and with ammunition. It is free through nonviolent means. Because of that the British Empire will not have the bitterness for Ghana that she has for China, so to speak. Because of that when the British Empire leaves Ghana, she leaves with a different attitude than she would have left with if she had been driven out by armies. We've got to revolt in such a way that after revolt is over we can live with people as their brothers and their sisters. Our aim must never be to defeat them or humiliate them.

On the night of the State Ball, standing up talking with some people, Mordecai Johnson called my attention to the fact that Prime Minister Kwame Nkrumah was there dancing with the duchess of Kent. And I said, "Isn't this something? Here is the once-serf, the once-slave, now dancing with the lord on an equal plane." And that is done because there is no bitterness. These two nations will be able to live together and work together because the breaking aloose was through nonviolence and not through violence.

The aftermath of nonviolence is the creation of the beloved community. The aftermath of nonviolence is redemption. The aftermath of nonviolence is reconciliation. The aftermath of violence are emptiness and bitterness. This is the thing I'm concerned about. Let us fight passionately and unrelentingly for the goals of justice and peace. But let's be sure that our hands are clean in this struggle. Let us never fight with falsehood and violence and hate and malice, but always fight with love, so that, when the day comes that the walls of segregation have completely crumbled in Montgomery, that we will be able to live with people as their brothers and sisters. Oh, my friends, our aim must be not to defeat Mr. Engelhardt, not to defeat Mr. Sellers and Mr. Gayle and Mr. Parks. Our aim must be to defeat the evil that's in them. But our aim must be to win the friendship of Mr. Gayle and Mr. Sellers and Mr. Engelhardt. We must come to the point of seeing that our ultimate aim is to live with all men as brothers and sisters under God, and not be their enemies or anything that goes with that type of relationship. And this is one thing that Ghana teaches us: that you can break aloose from evil through nonviolence, through a lack of bitterness. Nkrumah says in his book: "When I came out of prison, I was not bitter toward Britain. I came out merely with the determination to free my people from the colonialism and imperialism that had been inflicted upon them by the British. But I came out with no bitterness." And, because of that, this world will be a better place in which to live.

There's another thing that Ghana reminds us. I'm coming to the conclusion now. Ghana reminds us that freedom never comes on a silver platter. It's never easy. Ghana reminds us that whenever you break out of Egypt, you better get ready for stiff backs. You better get ready for some homes to be bombed. You better get ready for some churches to be bombed. You better get ready for a lot of nasty things to be said about you, because you getting out of Egypt. And whenever you break aloose from Egypt, the initial response of the Egyptian is bitterness. It never comes with ease. It comes only through the hardness and persistence of life. Ghana reminds us of that. You better get ready to go to prison. When I looked out and saw the prime minister there with his prison cap on that night, that reminded me of that fact, that freedom never comes easy. It comes through hard labor and it comes through toil. It comes through hours of despair and disappointment.

And that's the way it goes. There is no crown without a cross. I wish we could get to Easter without going to Good Friday, but history tells us that we got to go by Good Friday before we can get to Easter. That's the long story of freedom, isn't it? Before you get to Canaan, you've got a Red Sea to confront. You have a hardened heart of a pharaoh to confront. You have the prodigious hilltops of evil in the wilderness to confront. And even when you get up to the Promised Land, you have giants in the land. The beautiful thing about it is that there are a few people who've been over in the land. They have spied enough to say, "Even though the giants are there we can possess the land, because we got the internal fiber to stand up amid anything that we have to face."

The road to freedom is a difficult, hard road. It always makes for temporary setbacks. And those people who tell you today that there is more tension in Montgomery than there has ever been are telling you right. Whenever you get out of Egypt, you always confront a little tension, you always confront a little temporary setback. If you didn't confront that you'd never get out. You must remember that the tensionless period that we like to think of was the period when the Negro was complacently adjusted to segregation, discrimination, insult, and exploitation. And the period of tension is the period when the Negro has decided to rise up and break aloose from that. And this is the peace that we are seeking: not an old negative obnoxious peace which is merely the absence of tension, but a positive, lasting peace, which is the presence of brotherhood and justice. And it is never brought about without this temporary period of tension.

The road to freedom is difficult, but finally, Ghana tells us that the forces of the universe are on the side of justice. That's what it tells us, now. You can interpret Ghana any kind of way you want to, but Ghana tells me that the forces of the universe are on the side of justice. That night when I saw that old flag coming down and the new flag coming up, I saw something else. That wasn't just an ephemeral, evanescent event appearing on the stage of history. But it was an event with eternal meaning, for it symbolizes something. That thing symbolized to me that an old order is passing away and a new order is coming into being. An old order of colonialism, of segregation, of discrimination is passing away now. And a new order of justice and freedom and goodwill is being born. That's what it said. Somehow the forces of justice stand on the side of the universe, and that you can't ultimately trample over God's children and profit by it.

I want to come back to Montgomery now, but I must stop by London for a moment. For London reminds me of something. I never will forget the day we went into London. The next day we started moving around this great city, the only city in the world that is almost as large as New York City. Over eight million people in London, about eight million, three hundred thousand; New York about eight million, five hundred thousand. London larger in area than New York, though. Standing in London is an amazing picture. And I never will forget the experience I had, the thoughts that came to my mind. We went to Buckingham Palace. And I looked there at all of Britain, at all of the pomp and circumstance of royalty. And I thought about all of the queens and kings that had passed through here. Look at the beauty of the changing of the guards and all of the guards with their beautiful horses. It's a beautiful sight. Move on from there and go over to Parliament. Move into the House of Lords and the House of Commons. There with all of its beauty standing up before the world is one of the most beautiful sights in the world.

Then I remember, we went on over to Westminster Abbey. And I thought about several things when we went in this great church, this great cathedral, the center of the Church of England. We walked around and went to the tombs of the kings and queens buried there. Most of the kings and queens of England are buried right there in the Westminster Abbey. And I walked around. On the one hand I enjoyed and appreciated the great gothic architecture of that massive cathedral. I stood there in awe thinking about the greatness of God and man's feeble attempt to reach up for God. And I thought something else. I thought about the Church of England. My mind went back to Buckingham Palace, and I said that this is the symbol of a dying system. There was a day that the queens and kings of England could boast that the sun never sets on the British Empire. A day when she occupied the greater portion of Australia, the greater portion of Canada. There was a day when she ruled most of China, most of Africa, and all of India. I started thinking about this empire.

I started thinking about the fact that she ruled over India one day. Mahatma Gandhi stood there at every hand, trying to get the freedom of his people. And they never bowed to it. They never, they decided that they were going to stand up and hold India in humiliation and in colonialism many, many years. I remember we passed by Ten Downing Street. That's the place where the prime minister of England lives. And I remember that a few years ago a man lived there by the name of Winston Churchill. One day he stood up before the world and said, "I did not become His Majesty's first minister to preside over the liquidation of the British Empire."

And I thought about the fact that a few weeks ago a man by the name of Anthony Eden lived there. And out of all of his knowledge of the Middle East, he decided to rise up and march his armies with the forces of Israel and France into Egypt. And there they confronted their doom, because they were revolting against world opinion. Egypt, a little country. Egypt, a country with no military power. They could have easily defeated Egypt. But they did not realize that they were fighting more than Egypt. They were attacking world opinion, they were fighting the whole Asian-African bloc, which is the bloc that now thinks and moves and determines the course of the history of the world.

I thought of many things. I thought of the fact that the British Empire exploited India. Think about it! A nation with four hundred million people and the British exploited them so much that out of a population of four hundred million, three hundred and fifty million made an annual income of less than fifty dollars a year. Twenty-five of that had to be used for taxes and the other things of life. I thought about dark Africa. And how the people there, if they can make a hundred dollars a year they are living very well they think. Two shillings a day—one shilling is fourteen cents, two shillings, twenty-eight cents—that's a good wage. That's because of the domination of the British Empire.

All of these things came to my mind, and when I stood there in Westminster Abbey with all of its beauty, and I thought about all of the beautiful hymns and anthems that the people would go in there to sing. And yet the Church of England never took a stand against this system. The Church of England sanctioned it. The Church of England gave it moral stature. All of the exploitation perpetuated by the British Empire was sanctioned by the Church of England.

But something else came to my mind. God comes in the picture even when the Church won't take a stand. God has injected a principle in this universe. God has said that all men must respect the dignity and worth of all human personality, "And if you don't do that, I will take charge." It seems this morning that I can hear God speaking. I can hear Him speaking throughout the universe, saying, "Be still and know that I am God. And if you don't stop, if you don't straighten up, if you don't stop exploiting people, I'm going to rise up and break the backbone of your power. And your power will be no more!" And the power of Great Britain is no more. I looked at France. I looked at Britain. And I thought about the Britain that could boast, "The sun never sets on our great Empire." And I said now she had gone to the level that the sun hardly rises on the British Empire. Because it was based on exploitation. Because the God of the universe eventually takes a stand.

And I say to you this morning, my friends, rise up and know that, as you struggle for justice, you do not struggle alone. But God struggles with you. And He is working every day. Somehow I can look out, I can look out across the seas and across the universe, and cry out, "Mine eyes have seen the glory of the coming of the Lord. He is trampling out the vintage where the grapes of wrath are stored." Then I think about it because His truth is marching on, and I can sing another chorus: "Hallelujah, glory hallelujah! His truth is marching on."

Then I can hear Isaiah again, because it has profound meaning to me, that somehow "every valley shall be exalted, and every hill shall be made low; the crooked places shall be made straight, and the rough places plain; and the glory of the Lord shall be revealed, and all flesh shall see it together."

That's the beauty of this thing: all flesh shall see it together. Not some from the heights of Park Street and others from the dungeons of slum areas. Not some from the pinnacles of the British Empire and some from the dark deserts of Africa. Not some from inordinate, superfluous wealth and others from abject, deadening poverty. Not some white and not some black, not some yellow and not some brown, but all flesh shall see it together. They shall see it from Montgomery. They shall see it from New York. They shall see it from Ghana. They shall see it from China.

For I can look out and see a great number, as John saw, marching into the great eternity, because God is working in this world, and at this hour, and at this moment. And God grants that we will get on board and start marching with God because we got orders now to break down the bondage and the walls of colonialism, exploitation, and imperialism. To break them down to the point that no man will trample over another man, but that all men will respect the dignity and worth of all human personality. And then we will be in Canaan's freedom land.

Moses might not get to see Canaan, but his children will see it. He even got to the mountain top enough to see it and that assured him that it was coming. But the beauty of the thing is that there's always a Joshua to take up his work and take the children on in. And it's there waiting with its milk and honey, and with all of the bountiful beauty that God has in store for His children. Oh, what exceedingly marvelous things God has in store for us. Grant that we will follow Him enough to gain them. [*Recording interrupted*]

O God, our gracious Heavenly Father, help us to

see the insights that come from this new nation. Help us to follow Thee and all of Thy creative works in this world. And that somehow we will discover that we are made to live together as brothers. And that it will come in this generation: the day when all men will recognize the fatherhood of God and the brotherhood of man. Amen.

DELIVERED AT DEXTER AVENUE BAPTIST CHURCH,
MONTGOMERY, ALABAMA,
7 APRIL 1957.

GIVE US THE BALLOT

INTRODUCTION BY THE HONORABLE
WALTER E. FAUNTROY

On May 17, 1957, the NAACP celebrated the third anniversary of the historic 1954 Supreme Court decision that struck down the policy of racial segregation in our nation's public schools with a Prayer Pilgrimage for Freedom at the Lincoln Memorial. A native of Washington, D.C., completing my junior year at Yale Divinity School, I was in attendance on that beautiful spring day when Dr. Martin Luther King, Jr., shared with the world his profound understanding of the political process in our great democracy.

As the director of the Southern Christian Leadership Conference's Washington Bureau, it was my privilege to work closely with Dr. King for eight years. From those years, a particular lesson has stayed with me always: He taught me the two definitions of politics that have thereafter guided my activities, both in the streets of America and in the suites of the United States Congress.

First, politics is the process by which we in a democracy create laws from our beliefs. Second, politics is the process of determining who gets how much of the whats, whens, wheres, and hows in five areas: income, education, health care, housing, and justice.

Dr. King realized that state-sanctioned racial segregation in the eleven southern states had become public policy because millions of the African-American citizens of the Southland had been blatantly and brutally denied the right to vote. Those who *did* vote saw their beliefs—that all people are *not* created equal—translated into public policy, and that policy gave less income, education, health care, housing, and justice to the African-American.

On that bright spring day in 1957, at a time when civil rights activists were focused upon the efficacy of action in the courts, the prayer rooms, and the streets of America, Dr. King pointed the way to the efficacy of action in the *voting booths*. If we go to the polls to vote, he said, then we can elect people who understand our beliefs—*and* who will create public policy and practice from that understanding. And the vote gives us power: We have a say in what goes where, and how, in those five essential elements of living.

"Give us the ballot," he said.

Blessedly, in the more than four decades since Dr. King pointed us to the voting booths, we have seen much of his wisdom in this regard bear fruit. I like to think that from that podium on the steps of the Lincoln Memorial he envisioned a day when—four million new black voters from the Southland later—the number of black elected officials would rise from only six hundred nationwide to over eight thousand. A day when we would have nearly forty black members of the U.S. House of Representatives, and African-Americans would occupy positions in the president's cabinet—positions as varied as the secretary of commerce, agriculture, energy, transportation, labor, and the Army.

Wow! What a vision! As you read this potent and perceptive speech, create another vision—this time of what we can do in the arena of public policy in the twenty-first century, a vision that brings "good news to the poor, that binds up the brokenhearted and that sets at liberty them that are bound." And to realize that vision, we only need to utilize the ballot that was made powerful as a result of the life and work of our beloved Dr. Martin Luther King, Jr. Then, and only then, may we go forth, take action, and transform his once-impossible dreams into living realities.

WALTER E. FAUNTROY was head of the Washington, D.C., affiliate of the Southern Christian Leadership Conference, and helped coordinate the August 28, 1963, March on Washington for Jobs and Freedom. In 1971 Fauntroy became the District of Columbia's first elected representative to the United States Congress in a century. He is currently president of the National Black Leadership Roundtable.

GIVE US
THE
BALLOT

M r. Chairman, distinguished platform associates, fellow Americans: Three years ago the Supreme Court of this nation rendered in simple, eloquent, and unequivocal language a decision which will long be stenciled on the mental sheets of succeeding generations. For all men of goodwill, this May seventeenth decision came as a joyous daybreak to end the long night of human captivity. It came as a great beacon light of hope to millions of disinherited people throughout the world who had dared only to dream of freedom.

Unfortunately, this noble and sublime decision has not gone without opposition. This opposition has often risen to ominous proportions. Many states have risen up in open defiance. The legislative halls of the South ring loud with such words as "interposition" and "nullification."

But even more, all types of conniving methods are still being used to prevent Negroes from becoming registered voters. The denial of this sacred right is a tragic betrayal of the highest mandates of our democratic tradition. And so our most urgent request to the president of the United States and every member of Congress is to give us the right to vote. [*Audience:*] (*Yes*)

Give us the ballot, and we will no longer have to worry the federal government about our basic rights.

Give us the ballot (*Yes*), and we will no longer plead to the federal government for passage of an anti-lynching law; we will by the power of our vote write the law on the statute books of the South (*All right*) and bring an end to the dastardly acts of the hooded perpetrators of violence.

Give us the ballot (*Give us the ballot*), and we will transform the salient misdeeds of bloodthirsty mobs (*Yeah*) into the calculated good deeds of orderly citizens.

Give us the ballot (*Give us the ballot*), and we will fill our legislative halls with men of goodwill (*All right now*) and send to the sacred halls of Congress men who will not sign a "Southern Manifesto" because of their devotion to the manifesto of justice. (*Tell 'em about it*)

Give us the ballot (*Yeah*), and we will place judges on the benches of the South who will do justly and love mercy (*Yeah*), and we will place at the head of the southern states governors who will, who have felt not only the tang of the human, but the glow of the Divine.

Give us the ballot (*Yes*), and we will quietly and nonviolently, without rancor or bitterness, implement the Supreme Court's decision of May seventeenth, 1954. (*That's right*)

In this juncture of our nation's history, there is an

urgent need for dedicated and courageous leadership. If we are to solve the problems ahead and make racial justice a reality, this leadership must be fourfold.

First, there is need for strong, aggressive leadership from the federal government. So far, only the judicial branch of the government has evinced this quality of leadership. If the executive and legislative branches of the government were as concerned about the protection of our citizenship rights as the federal courts have been, then the transition from a segregated to an integrated society would be infinitely smoother. But we so often look to Washington in vain for this concern. In the midst of the tragic breakdown of law and order, the executive branch of the government is all too silent and apathetic. In the midst of the desperate need for civil rights legislation, the legislative branch of the government is all too stagnant and hypocritical.

This dearth of positive leadership from the federal government is not confined to one particular political party. Both political parties have betrayed the cause of justice. (*Oh yes*) The Democrats have betrayed it by capitulating to the prejudices and undemocratic practices of the southern Dixiecrats. The Republicans have betrayed it by capitulating to the blatant hypocrisy of right-wing, reactionary northerners. These men so often have a high blood pressure of words and an anemia of deeds. [*Laughter*]

In the midst of these prevailing conditions, we come to Washington today pleading with the president and members of Congress to provide a strong, moral, and courageous leadership for a situation that cannot permanently be evaded. We come humbly to say to the men in the forefront of our government that the civil rights issue is not an ephemeral, evanescent domestic issue that can be kicked about by reactionary guardians of the status quo; it is rather an eternal moral issue which may well determine the destiny of our nation (*Yeah*) in the ideological struggle with communism. The hour is late. The clock of destiny is ticking out. We must act now, before it is too late.

A second area in which there is need for strong leadership is from the white northern liberals. There is a dire need today for a liberalism which is truly liberal. What we are witnessing today in so many northern communities is a sort of quasi-liberalism which is based on the principle of looking sympathetically at all sides. It is a liberalism so bent on seeing all sides, that it fails to become committed to either side. It is a liberalism that is so objectively analytical that it is not subjectively committed. It is a liberalism which is neither hot nor cold, but lukewarm. (*All right*) We call for a liberalism from the North which will be thoroughly committed to the ideal of racial justice and will not be deterred by the propaganda and subtle words of those who say: "Slow up for a while; you're pushing too fast."

A third source that we must look to for strong leadership is from the moderates of the white South. It is unfortunate that at this time the leadership of the white South stems from the close-minded reactionaries. These persons gain prominence and power by the dissemination of false ideas and by deliberately appealing to the deepest hate responses within the human mind. It is my firm belief that this close-minded, reactionary, recalcitrant group constitutes a numerical minority. There are in the white South more open-minded moderates than appears on the surface. These persons are silent today because of fear of social, political, and economic reprisals. God grant that the white moderates of the South will rise up courageously, without fear, and take up the leadership in this tense period of transition.

I cannot close without stressing the urgent need for strong, courageous, and intelligent leadership from the Negro community. We need a leadership that is calm and yet positive. This is no day for the rabble-rouser, whether he be Negro or white. (*All right*) We must realize that we are grappling with the most weighty social problem of this nation, and in grappling with such a complex problem there is no place for misguided emotionalism. (*All right, That's right*) We must work passionately and unrelentingly for the goal of freedom, but we must be sure that our hands are clean in the struggle. We must never struggle with falsehood, hate, or malice. We must never become bitter. I know how we feel sometime. There is the danger that those of us who have been forced so long to stand amid the tragic midnight of oppression—those of us who have been trampled over, those of us who have been kicked about—there is the danger that we will become bitter. But if we will become bitter and indulge in hate campaigns, the old, the new order which is emerging will be nothing but a duplication of the old order. (*Yeah, That's all right*)

We must meet hate with love. We must meet physical force with soul force. (*Yeah*) There is still a voice crying out through the vista of time, saying: "Love your enemies (*Yeah*), bless them that curse you (*Yes*), pray for them that despitefully use you." (*That's right, All right*) Then, and only then, can you matriculate into the university of eternal life. That same voice cries out in terms lifted to cosmic proportions: "He who lives by the sword will perish by the sword." (*Yeah, Lord*) And history is replete with the bleached bones of nations (*Yeah*) that failed to follow this command. (*All right*) We must follow nonviolence and love. (*Yes, Lord*)

Now, I'm not talking about a sentimental, shallow kind of love. (*Go ahead*) I'm not talking about *eros*, which is a sort of aesthetic, romantic love. I'm not even talking about *philia*, which is a sort of intimate affection between personal friends. But I'm talking about *agape*. (*Yes sir*) I'm talking about the love of God in the hearts of men. (*Yes*) I'm talking about a type of love which will cause you to love the person who does the evil deed while hating the deed that the person does. (*Go ahead*) We've got to love. (*Oh yes*)

There is another warning signal. We talk a great deal about our rights, and rightly so. We proudly proclaim that three-fourths of the peoples of the world are colored. We have the privilege of noticing in our generation the great drama of freedom and independence as it unfolds in Asia and Africa. All of these things are in line with the unfolding work of Providence. But we must be sure that we accept them in the right spirit. We must not seek to use our emerging freedom and our growing power to do the same thing to the white minority that has been done to us for so many centuries. (*Yes*) Our aim must never be to defeat or humiliate the white man. We must not become victimized with a philosophy of black supremacy. God is not interested merely in freeing black men and brown men and yellow men, but God is interested in freeing the whole human race. (*Yes, All right*) We must work with determination to create a society (*Yes*), not where black men are superior and other men are inferior and vice versa, but a society in which all men will live together as brothers (*Yes*) and respect the dignity and worth of human personality. (*Yes*)

We must also avoid the temptation of being victimized with a psychology of victors. We have won marvelous victories. Through the work of the NAACP, we have been able to do some of the most amazing things of this generation. And I come this afternoon with nothing, nothing but praise for this great organization, the work that it has already done and the work that it will do in the future. And although they're outlawed in Alabama and other states, the fact still remains that this organization has done more to achieve civil rights for Negroes than any other organization we can point to. (*Yeah, Amen*) Certainly, this is fine.

But we must not, however, remain satisfied with a court victory over our white brothers. We must respond to every decision with an understanding of those who have opposed us and with an appreciation of the difficult adjustments that the court orders pose for them. We must act in such a way as to make possible a coming together of white people and colored people on the basis of a real harmony of interest and understanding. We must seek an integration based on mutual respect.

I conclude by saying that each of us must keep faith in the future. Let us not despair. Let us realize that as we struggle for justice and freedom, we have cosmic companionship. This is the long faith of the Hebraic-Christian tradition: that God is not some Aristotelian "unmoved mover" who merely contemplates upon Himself. He is not merely a self-knowing God, but an other-loving God (*Yeah*) forever working through history for the establishment of His kingdom.

And those of us who call the name of Jesus Christ find something of an event in our Christian faith that tells us this. There is something in our faith that says to us, "Never despair; never give up; never feel that the cause of righteousness and justice is doomed." There is something in our Christian faith, at the center of it, which says to us that Good Friday may occupy the throne for a day, but ultimately it must give way to the triumphant beat of the drums of Easter. (*That's right*) There is something in our faith that says evil may so shape events, that Caesar will occupy the palace and Christ the cross (*That's right*), but one day that same Christ will rise up and split history into A.D. and B.C. (*Yes*), so that even the name, the life of Caesar must be dated by his name. (*Yes*) There is something in this universe (*Yes, Yes*) which justifies Carlyle in saying: "No lie can live forever." (*All right*) There is something in this universe which justifies William Cullen Bryant in saying: "Truth crushed to earth will rise again." (*Yes, All right*) There is something in this universe (*Watch yourself*) which justifies James Russell Lowell in saying:

> Truth forever on the scaffold,
> Wrong forever on the throne. (*Oh yeah*)
> Yet that scaffold sways the future,
> And behind the dim unknown
> Stands God (*All right*), within the shadow,
> Keeping watch above His own. (*Yeah, Yes*)

Go out with that faith today. (*All right, Yes*) Go back to your homes in the Southland to that faith, with that faith today. Go back to Philadelphia, to New York, to Detroit and Chicago with that faith today (*That's right*), that the universe is on our side in the struggle. (*Sure is, Yes*) Stand up for justice. (*Yes*) Sometimes it gets hard, but it is always difficult to get out of Egypt, for the Red Sea always stands before you with discouraging dimensions. (*Yes*) And even after you've crossed the Red Sea, you have to move through a wilderness with prodigious hilltops of evil (*Yes*) and gigantic mountains of opposition. (*Yes*) But I say to you this afternoon: Keep moving. (*Go on ahead*) Let nothing slow you up. (*Go on ahead*) Move on with dignity and honor and respectability. (*Yes*)

I realize that it will cause restless nights sometimes. It might cause losing a job; it will cause suffering and sacrifice. (*That's right*) It might even cause physical death for some. But if physical death is the price that some must pay (*Yes sir*) to free their children from a permanent life of psychological death (*Yes sir*), then nothing can be more Christian. (*Yes sir*) Keep going today. (*Yes sir*) Keep moving amid every obstacle. (*Yes sir*) Keep moving amid every mountain of opposition. (*Yes sir, Yeah*) If you will do that with dignity (*Say it*), when the history books are written in the future, the historians will have to look back and say, "There lived a great people. (*Yes sir, Yes*) A people with 'fleecy locks and black complexion,' but a people who injected new meaning into the veins of civilization (*Yes*); a people which stood up with dignity and honor and saved Western civilization in her darkest hour (*Yes*); a people that gave new integrity and a new dimension of love to our civilization." (*Yeah, Look out*) When that happens, the morning stars will sing together (*Yes sir*), and the sons of God will shout for joy. (*Yes sir, All right*) [*Applause*] (*Yes, That's wonderful, All right*)

DELIVERED AT THE PRAYER PILGRIMAGE FOR FREEDOM,
WASHINGTON, D.C.,
17 MAY 1957.

ADDRESS AT THE FREEDOM RALLY IN COBO HALL

INTRODUCTION BY ARETHA AND ERMA FRANKLIN

In May of 1963, I had the great privilege of following Mahalia Jackson and Dinah Washington in closing out a benefit concert at Chicago's Wrigley Field for the Civil Rights Movement's Birmingham Campaign, one of many concerts in which I participated with Dr. King.

It was a wonderful experience for a young singer (I was twenty-one), and I was elated to have the chance to make a contribution to such a great and noble cause. Shortly thereafter, my father, the Reverend C. L. Franklin, one of Detroit's and the nation's leading clergymen and civil rights activists, invited Dr. King to lead a mass march and speak at a rally in our city. My father hoped that this event would lay the foundation for creating a higher local level of consciousness for the Civil Rights Movement and for his organization, the Detroit Human Rights Commission, and its affiliate, the Southern Christian Leadership Conference.

The Detroit march was set for June 23, culminating in a rally at the downtown Cobo Hall. The march was a huge success, and the crowd was so enthusiastic that, at one point, Dr. King, my father, Ben McFall, Walter Reuther, and Mayor Cavanaugh were literally swept off their feet as they linked arms at the front of the march when the crowd, swelling to over 150,000 people, surged forward. Dr. King called it the largest and greatest demonstration for freedom ever held in the United States.

As a minister's daughter, I had heard many discussions among preachers about the oratorical skills of different clergymen. But after Dr. King's speech at Cobo Hall that day, there was another standard of eloquence.

The history books say that Dr. King's speech on that day set the stage for his "I Have a Dream" speech at the great March on Washington later that summer. And indeed, Dr. King did explore some of the themes and language he would use at the Lincoln Memorial. But on that magical day, we knew that Detroit had been blessed with a tremendous vision of unity and brother- and sisterhood that had never been so well articulated and organized in America, and that somehow things were going to change for the better. Dr. King began by thanking my father and members of the Human Rights Commission of the Detroit march, which he said would serve as a source of inspiration for freedom-loving people of this nation. He commended all of the march's participants and local leadership for keeping faith with nonviolence.

The massive crowd roared in Cobo Hall when he

told them that the message of the recently triumphant Birmingham campaign was that we are through with segregation now, henceforth, and forever more. He spoke of the awakening consciousness of black Americans on the march to full equality. As a singer living in what was then considered the unrivaled capital of American popular music, I especially appreciated Dr. King's lyrical assurance that every man from a bass black to a treble white is significant on God's keyboard.

There are a number of such themes and phrases to be found in Dr. King's great "I Have a Dream" speech, and he previewed in Detroit some of the themes he would later use in other speeches. He spoke about the power of soul and how nonviolent resistance could transform jails from dungeons of shame to havens of freedom and human dignity. He spoke about the more subtle character of northern racism and the futility of black separatism, and he called on the marchers to join him in Washington, D.C., on August 28 for another mass march to help pass the civil rights bill.

Dr. King's Detroit address can stand on its own as a masterpiece of public oration. I know that for many months afterward, everyone who was there and heard the sound of his voice at Cobo Hall had his inspirational message of hope for the future reflected in his or her face. So, come and travel with me now, back down the vista of the past, and let us read these timeless words, knowing that Dr. King's teachings about truth, justice, love, and equality will forever stand and light the way to liberation for all humanity.

God Bless this great man of God.

* * *

ARETHA and ERMA FRANKLIN grew up in the home of one of Detroit's leading clergymen and civil rights activists, their father, C. L. Franklin. Aretha began her career as a gospel singer at churches and civil rights rallies, and later became known to many as the "Queen of Soul." Dr. King praised her in 1967 as a "devoted and consistent supporter" of the cause of freedom.

ADDRESS AT THE
FREEDOM RALLY IN
COBO HALL

My good friend, the Reverend C. L. Franklin, and all of the officers and members of the Detroit Council of Human Rights, distinguished platform guests, ladies and gentlemen: I cannot begin to say to you this afternoon how thrilled I am, and I cannot begin to tell you the deep joy that comes to my heart as I participate with you in what I consider the largest and greatest demonstration for freedom ever held in the United States. [*Applause*] And I can assure you that what has been done here today will serve as a source of inspiration for all of the freedom-loving people of this nation. [*Audience:*] (*All right*) [*Applause*]

I think there is something else that must be said because it is a magnificent demonstration of discipline. With all of the thousands and hundreds of thousands of people engaged in this demonstration today, there has not been one reported incident of violence. [*Applause*] I think this is a magnificent demonstration of our commitment to nonviolence in this struggle for freedom all over the United States, and I want to commend the leadership of this community for making this great event possible and making such a great event possible through such disciplined channels. [*Applause*]

Almost one hundred and one years ago, on September the twenty-second, 1862, to be exact, a great and noble American, Abraham Lincoln, signed an executive order, which was to take effect on January the first, 1863. This executive order was called the Emancipation Proclamation and it served to free the Negro from the bondage of physical slavery. But one hundred years later, the Negro in the United States of America still isn't free. [*Applause*]

But now more than ever before, America is forced to grapple with this problem, for the shape of the world today does not afford us the luxury of an anemic democracy. And the price that this nation must pay for the continued oppression and exploitation of the Negro or any other minority group is the price of its own destruction. For the hour is late, and the clock of destiny is ticking out, and we must act now before it is too late. (*Yeah*) [*Applause*]

The events of Birmingham, Alabama, and the more than sixty communities that have started protest movements since Birmingham, are indicative of the fact that the Negro is now determined to be free. (*Yeah*) [*Applause*] For Birmingham tells us something in glaring terms. It says first that the Negro is no longer willing to accept racial segregation in any of its dimensions. [*Applause*] For we have come to see that segregation is not only sociologically untenable, it is not only politically unsound, it is morally wrong and sinful. Segregation is a cancer in the body politic, which must be removed before our democratic health can be realized. (*Yeah*) [*Applause*] Segregation is wrong because it is nothing but a new form of slavery covered up with certain niceties of complexity. [*Applause*] Segregation is wrong because it is a system of adultery perpetuated by an illicit intercourse between injustice and immorality. [*Applause*] And in Birmingham, Alabama, and all over the South and all over the nation, we are simply saying that we will no longer sell our birthright of freedom for a mess of segregated pottage. (*All right*) [*Applause*] In a real sense, we are through with segregation now, henceforth, and forevermore. [*Sustained applause*]

Now Birmingham and the freedom struggle tell us something else. (*Talk*) They reveal to us that the Negro has a new sense of dignity and a new sense of self-respect. (*Yes*) For years (*That's right, Come a long way*) [*Applause*]—I think we will all agree that probably the most damaging effect of segregation has been what it has done to the soul of the segregated as well as the segregator. [*Applause*] It has given the segregator a false sense of superiority and it has left the segregated with a false sense of inferiority. (*All right*) [*Applause*] And so because of the legacy of slavery and segregation, many Negroes lost faith in themselves and many felt that they were inferior.

But then something happened to the Negro. Circumstances made it possible and necessary for him to travel more: the coming of the automobile, the upheavals of two world wars, the Great Depression. And so his rural, plantation background gradually gave way to urban, industrial life. And even his economic life was rising through the growth of industry, the influence of organized labor, expanded educational opportunities. And even his cultural life was rising through the steady decline of crippling illiteracy. And all of these forces conjoined to cause the Negro to take a new look at himself. Negro masses [*Applause*], Negro masses all over began to reevaluate themselves, and the Negro came to feel that he was somebody. His religion revealed to him [*Laughter, applause*], his religion revealed to him that God loves all of His children, and that all men are made in His image, and that figuratively speaking, every man from a bass black to a treble white is significant on God's keyboard. [*Applause*]

So, the Negro can now unconsciously cry out with the eloquent poet:

Fleecy locks and black complexion
Cannot forfeit nature's claim.
Skin may differ, but affection
Dwells in black and white the same.
Were I so tall as to reach the pole
Or to grasp at the ocean at a span,
I must be measured by my soul
The mind is the standard of the man. [*Applause*]

But these events that are taking place in our nation tell us something else. They tell us that the Negro and his allies in the white community now recognize the urgency of the moment. I know we have heard a lot of cries saying, "Slow up" and "Cool off." [*Laughter*] We still hear these cries. They are telling us over and over again that you're pushing things too fast, and so they're saying, "Cool off." Well, the only answer that we can give to that is that we've cooled off all too long, and there is the danger [*Applause*], there's always the danger if you cool off too much that you will end up in a deep freeze. [*Applause*] "Well," they're saying, "you need to put on brakes." The only answer that we can give to that is that the motor's now cranked up and we're moving up the highway of freedom toward the city of equality [*Applause*], and we can't afford to stop now because our nation has a date with destiny. We must keep moving.

Then there is another cry. They say, "Why don't you do it in a gradual manner?" Well, gradualism is little more than escapism and do-nothingism, which ends up in stand-stillism. [*Applause*] We know that our brothers and sisters in Africa and Asia are moving with jetlike speed toward the goal of political independence. And in some communities we are still moving at horse-and-buggy pace toward the gaining of a hamburger and a cup of coffee at a lunch counter. [*Applause*]

And so we must say: Now is the time to make real the promises of democracy. Now is the time to transform this pending national elegy into a creative psalm of brotherhood. Now is the time to lift our nation [*Applause*], now is the time to lift our nation from the quicksands of racial injustice to the solid rock of racial justice. Now is the time to get rid of segregation and discrimination. Now is the time. (*Now, Now*) [*Applause*]

And so this social revolution taking place can be

summarized in three little words. They are not big words. One does not need an extensive vocabulary to understand them. They are the words "all," "here," and "now." We want *all* of our rights, we want them *here*, and we want them *now*. This is the meaning. [*Applause*] [*Recording interrupted*]

Now the other thing that we must see about this struggle is that by and large it has been a nonviolent struggle. Let nobody make you feel that those who are engaged or who are engaging in the demonstrations in communities all across the South are resorting to violence; these are few in number. For we've come to see the power of nonviolence. We've come to see that this method is not a weak method, for it's the strong man who can stand up amid opposition, who can stand up amid violence being inflicted upon him and not retaliate with violence. (*Yeah*) [*Applause*]

You see, this method has a way of disarming the opponent. It exposes his moral defenses. It weakens his morale, and at the same time it works on his conscience, and he just doesn't know what to do. If he doesn't beat you, wonderful. If he beats you, you develop the quiet courage of accepting blows without retaliating. If he doesn't put you in jail, wonderful. Nobody with any sense likes to go to jail. But if he puts you in jail, you go in that jail and transform it from a dungeon of shame to a haven of freedom and human dignity. [*Applause*] And even if he tries to kill you (*He can't kill you*), you develop the inner conviction that there are some things so dear, some things so precious, some things so eternally true, that they are worth dying for. (*Yes*) [*Applause*] And I submit to you that if a man has not discovered something that he will die for, he isn't fit to live. [*Applause*]

This method has wrought wonders. As a result of the nonviolent Freedom Ride movement, segregation in public transportation has almost passed away absolutely in the South. As a result of the sit-in movement at lunch counters, more than 285 cities have now integrated their lunch counters in the South. I say to you, there is power in this method. [*Applause*]

And I think by following this approach it will also help us to go into the new age that is emerging with the right attitude. For nonviolence not only calls upon its adherents to avoid external physical violence, but it calls upon them to avoid internal violence of spirit. It calls on them to engage in that something called love. And I know it is difficult sometimes. When I say "love" at this point, I'm not talking about an affectionate emotion. (*All right*) It's nonsense to urge people, oppressed people, to love their oppressors in an affectionate sense. I'm talking about something much deeper. I'm talking about a sort of understanding, creative, redemptive goodwill for all men. [*Applause*]

We are coming to see now, the psychiatrists are saying to us, that many of the strange things that happen in the subconscience, many of the inner conflicts, are rooted in hate. And so they are saying, "Love or perish." But Jesus told us this long time ago, and I can still hear that voice crying through the vista of time, saying, "Love your enemies, bless them that curse you, pray for them that despitefully use you." And there is still a voice saying to every potential

Peter, "Put up your sword." History is replete with the bleached bones of nations; history is cluttered with the wreckage of communities that failed to follow this command. And isn't it marvelous to have a method of struggle where it is possible to stand up against an unjust system, fight it with all of your might, never accept it, and yet not stoop to violence and hatred in the process? This is what we have. [*Applause*]

Now there is a magnificent new militancy within the Negro community all across this nation. And I welcome this as a marvelous development. The Negro of America is saying he's determined to be free and he is militant enough to stand up. But this new militancy must not lead us to the position of distrusting every white person who lives in the United States. There are some white people in this country who are as determined to see the Negro free as we are to be free. [*Applause*] This new militancy must be kept within understanding boundaries.

And then another thing I can understand. We've been pushed around so long; we've been the victims of lynching mobs so long; we've been the victims of economic injustice so long—still the last hired and the first fired all over this nation. And I know the temptation. I can understand from a psychological point of view why some caught up in the clutches of the injustices surrounding them almost respond with bitterness and come to the conclusion that the problem can't be solved within, and they talk about getting away from it in terms of racial separation. But even though I can understand it psychologically, I must say to you this afternoon that this isn't the way.

Black supremacy is as dangerous as white supremacy. [*Applause*] And oh, I hope you will allow me to say to you this afternoon that God is not interested merely in the freedom of black men and brown men and yellow men. God is interested in the freedom of the whole human race. [*Applause*] And I believe that with this philosophy and this determined struggle we will be able to go on in the days ahead and transform the jangling discords of our nation into a beautiful symphony of brotherhood.

As I move toward my conclusion, you're asking, I'm sure, "What can we do here in Detroit to help in the struggle in the South?" Well, there are several things that you can do. One of them you've done already, and I hope you will do it in even greater dimensions before we leave this meeting. [*Recording interrupted*]

Now the second thing that you can do to help us down in Alabama and Mississippi and all over the South is to work with determination to get rid of any segregation and discrimination in Detroit [*Applause*], realizing that injustice anywhere is a threat to justice everywhere. And we've got to come to see that the problem of racial injustice is a national problem. No community in this country can boast of clean hands in the area of brotherhood. Now in the North it's different in that it doesn't have the legal sanction that it has in the South. But it has its subtle and hidden forms and it exists in three areas: in the area of employment discrimination, in the area of housing discrimination, and in the area of de facto segregation in the public schools. And we must come to see that de facto segregation in the North is just as injurious of the, as the actual segregation in the South. [*Applause*] And so if you want to help us in Alabama and Mississippi and over the South, do all that you can to get rid of the problem here.

And then we also need your support in order to get the civil rights bill that the president is offering passed. And that's a reality, let's not fool ourselves: This bill isn't going to get through if we don't put some work in it and some determined pressure. And this is why I've said that in order to get this bill through, we've got to arouse the conscience of the nation, and we ought to march to Washington more than a hundred thousand in order to say [*Applause*], in order to say that we are determined, and in order to engage in a nonviolent protest to keep this issue before the conscience of the nation. And if we will do this we will be able to bring that new day of freedom into being. If we will do this we will be able to make the American dream a reality.

And I do not want to give you the impression that it's going to be easy. There can be no great social gain without individual pain. And before the victory for brotherhood is won, some will have to get scarred up a bit. Before the victory is won, some more will be thrown into jail. Before the victory is won, some, like Medgar Evers, may have to face physical death. But if physical death is the price that some must pay to free their children and their white brothers from an eternal psychological death, then nothing can be more redemptive. Before the victory is won, some will be misunderstood and called bad names, but we must go on with a determination and with a faith that this problem can be solved. (*Yeah*) [*Applause*]

And so I go back to the South not in despair. I go back to the South not with a feeling that we are caught in a dark dungeon that will never lead to a way out. I go back believing that the new day is coming. And so this afternoon, I have a dream. (*Go ahead*) It is a dream deeply rooted in the American dream.

I have a dream that one day, right down in Georgia and Mississippi and Alabama, the sons of former slaves and the sons of former slave owners will be able to live together as brothers.

I have a dream this afternoon (*I have a dream*) that one day [*Applause*], one day little white children and little Negro children will be able to join hands as brothers and sisters.

I have a dream this afternoon that one day [*Applause*], one day men will no longer burn down houses and the church of God simply because people want to be free.

I have a dream this afternoon (*I have a dream*) that there will be a day that we will no longer face the atrocities that Emmett Till had to face or Medgar Evers had to face, but that all men can live with dignity.

I have a dream this afternoon (*Yeah*) that my four little children, that my four little children will not come up in the same young days that I came up within, but they will be judged on the basis of the content of their character, and not the color of their skin. [*Applause*]

I have a dream this afternoon that one day right

here in Detroit, Negroes will be able to buy a house or rent a house anywhere that their money will carry them and they will be able to get a job. [*Applause*] (*That's right*)

Yes, I have a dream this afternoon that one day in this land the words of Amos will become real and justice will roll down like waters, and righteousness like a mighty stream.

I have a dream this evening that one day we will recognize the words of Jefferson that "all men are created equal, that they are endowed by their Creator with certain unalienable Rights, that among these are Life, Liberty and the pursuit of Happiness." I have a dream this afternoon. [*Applause*]

I have a dream that one day every valley shall be exalted, and every hill and mountain shall be made low; the rough places will be made plain, and the crooked places will be made straight; and the glory of the Lord shall be revealed, and all flesh shall see it together. [*Applause*]

I have a dream this afternoon that the brotherhood of man will become a reality in this day.

And with this faith I will go out and carve a tunnel of hope through the mountain of despair. With this faith, I will go out with you and transform dark yesterdays into bright tomorrows. With this faith, we will be able to achieve this new day when all of God's children, black men and white men, Jews and Gentiles, Protestants and Catholics, will be able to join hands and sing with the Negroes in the spiritual of old:

Free at last! Free at last!
Thank God Almighty, we are free at last! [*Applause*]

✦

DELIVERED IN DETROIT, MICHIGAN,
23 JUNE 1963.

I HAVE A DREAM

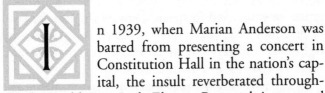

INTRODUCTION BY DR. DOROTHY I. HEIGHT

In 1939, when Marian Anderson was barred from presenting a concert in Constitution Hall in the nation's capital, the insult reverberated throughout the world. First Lady Eleanor Roosevelt intervened until arrangements were made for Marian Anderson to sing at the Lincoln Memorial.

On Easter Sunday, standing on the steps of the Lincoln Memorial, Marian Anderson sang and her first words were "My country 'tis of thee." The audience burst into thunderous applause. I thought I would never again witness a higher moment when the collective conscience of America was awakened. But I was wrong. Twenty-four years later Martin Luther King, Jr., stood on the steps of the Lincoln Memorial and, reciting from the anthem's first stanza, said, "From every mountainside, let freedom ring." It was a riveting sermon that struck the conscience of America, taking its place as one of the most famous speeches in human history.

Leading up to the march, there had been much discussion about who would speak and in what order. Women's groups wanted a female speaker included. Young people, especially the Student Nonviolent Coordinating Committee (SNCC), demanded a youth speaker. The women's demands were met with a refusal based on the notion that women were already represented as members of participating labor, faith-based, and civil rights groups. As it turned out, the only woman whose voice was heard was the great gospel singer Mahalia Jackson. Unlike the women, SNCC persisted in their demands and their representative was called to speak. Despite the intense level of give and take, there was a sense of unity fueled by righteous indignation that racial segregation and racism persisted in American society.

Many naturally assume that Dr. King initiated the March on Washington. In fact, it was an idea first conceived by A. Philip Randolph, the distinguished labor leader, whose threat of a similar march many years earlier had led to President Franklin D. Roosevelt's signing of Executive Order 8802 in 1941, which established the Fair Employment Practices Commission. By 1963, the country had broken faith and conditions were getting worse, rather than better. A. Philip Randolph deemed it time to issue a call for a march that would not be denied. A quarter of a million people answered the call. They came from all walks of life, all races, all income levels, all creeds . . . indeed, they came from all over the world. Buses by the hundreds converged on the nation's capital.

In anticipation of the march, there was great anxiety about the potential for rioting, bloodshed, and violent confrontation. President Kennedy remained aloof from it all. He would not meet with the march leaders. Roy Wilkins, of the NAACP, was chair of the United Civil Rights Leadership group, which organized a meeting with the police chief in the District of Columbia. Wilkins encouraged the chief to abandon any plans to use mounted police, knowing they would be perceived by the marchers as threatening.

To allay any fears about the temperament of the crowd, which would be marching on a hot summer day, Wilkins asked the question, "What shall we tell the people before they leave home?"

A burst of laughter and a sigh of relief greeted the chief's response.

"Tell them not to put any mayonnaise on their sandwiches," the chief said.

The day of the march there were so many people, from the reflecting pool to the base of the Lincoln Memorial, it was impossible to see the grass. People crammed into the space, eager to hear every word and see every speaker. When it was time for the last speech, Randolph, in his characteristically eloquent deep voice, presented with a flourish, "Martin Luther King, Jr.!"

Dr. King departed from his notes. He spoke from his heart. In retrospect, it was a brilliant decision to make him the final speaker, for no one could have followed his passionate and moving words. We listened to him as if he were speaking to each of us individually. I'm sure the applause and shouts and cheers that greeted his words could be heard for miles. It was a deeply spiritual experience.

As a young woman, I had been involved in the United Christian Youth Movement, organized to harness the optimism of Christian youth to build a new world. When I looked over the crowd as Dr. King finished his speech, I felt that, at last, we were all united in creating a new society. He had done more than deliver a speech. He had sent out a challenge to the world. It was as though he had seen into the hearts and souls of people everywhere and touched their deepest longing for a shared destiny, a common purpose, a sense of mission. He made us see how "We shall overcome, black and white together."

His message pointed out the country's glaring shortcomings—"America has given the Negro people a bad check, a check which has come back marked 'insufficient funds' "—yet he never sounded a negative note. He spoke with a vision of the beloved community. His commitment to love and peace through justice was evident.

For days and weeks and years afterward, the power of his words reached more and more people as radio and television stations all over the country played his speech at every opportunity.

It is a blessing that, through the efforts of Coretta Scott King, the essence of Martin Luther King, Jr.'s message has been institutionalized. Every King holiday, when the speech is broadcast, recited, or quoted, is a moment to remind us that King had a dream. But he was not assassinated for dreaming—he was assassinated because he dared to challenge the system.

The speech came from a soul force, a love and commitment to nonviolence that will continue to be relevant to the human experience.

DOROTHY I. HEIGHT served as president of the National Council of Negro Women from 1957 until 1998, and was one of the few female organizational leaders during the Civil Rights Movement. Height received the NAACP's prestigious Spingarn Medal in 1993, and was awarded the Presidential Medal of Freedom the following year.

I Have

A

Dream

I am happy to join with you today in what will go down in history as the greatest demonstration for freedom in the history of our nation. [*Applause*]

Fivescore years ago, a great American, in whose symbolic shadow we stand today, signed the Emancipation Proclamation. This momentous decree came as a great beacon light of hope to millions of Negro slaves who had been seared in the flames of withering injustice. It came as a joyous daybreak to end the long night of their captivity.

But one hundred years later, the Negro still is not free. [*Audience:*] (*My Lord*) One hundred years later, the life of the Negro is still sadly crippled by the manacles of segregation and the chains of discrimination. One hundred years later, the Negro lives on a lonely island of poverty in the midst of a vast ocean of material prosperity. One hundred years later (*My Lord*) [*Applause*], the Negro is still languished in the corners of American society and finds himself an exile in his own land. And so we've come here today to dramatize a shameful condition.

In a sense we've come to our nation's capital to cash

a check. When the architects of our republic wrote the magnificent words of the Constitution and the Declaration of Independence (*Yeah*), they were signing a promissory note to which every American was to fall heir. This note was a promise that all men, yes, black men as well as white men, would be guaranteed the "unalienable Rights of Life, Liberty, and the pursuit of Happiness." It is obvious today that America has defaulted on this promissory note insofar as her citizens of color are concerned. Instead of honoring this sacred obligation, America has given the Negro people a bad check, a check which has come back marked "insufficient funds." [*Sustained applause*]

But we refuse to believe that the bank of justice is bankrupt. (*My Lord*) [*Laughter*] (*Sure enough*) We refuse to believe that there are insufficient funds in the great vaults of opportunity of this nation. And so we've come to cash this check (*Yes*), a check that will give us upon demand the riches of freedom (*Yes*) and the security of justice. [*Applause*]

We have also come to this hallowed spot to remind America of the fierce urgency of now. This is no time (*My Lord*) to engage in the luxury of cooling off or to take the tranquilizing drug of gradualism. [*Applause*] Now is the time to make real the promises of democracy. (*My Lord*) Now is the time to rise from the dark and desolate valley of segregation to the sunlit path of racial justice. Now is the time [*Applause*] to lift our nation from the quicksands of racial injustice to the solid rock of brotherhood. Now is the time [*Applause*] to make justice a reality for all of God's children.

It would be fatal for the nation to overlook the urgency of the moment. This sweltering summer of the Negro's legitimate discontent will not pass until there is an invigorating autumn of freedom and equality. Nineteen sixty-three is not an end, but a beginning. And those who hope that the Negro needed to blow off steam and will now be content will have a rude awakening if the nation returns to business as usual. [*Applause*] There will be neither rest nor tranquillity in America until the Negro is granted his citizenship rights. The whirlwinds of revolt will continue to shake the foundations of our nation until the bright day of justice emerges.

But there is something that I must say to my people, who stand on the warm threshold which leads into the palace of justice: In the process of gaining our rightful place, we must not be guilty of wrongful deeds. Let us not seek to satisfy our thirst for freedom by drinking from the cup of bitterness and hatred. (*My Lord*) [*Applause*] We must forever conduct our struggle on the high plane of dignity and discipline. We must not allow our creative protest to degenerate into physical violence. Again and again, we must rise to the majestic heights of meeting physical force with soul force. The marvelous new militancy which has engulfed the Negro community must not lead us to a distrust of all white people, for many of our white brothers, as evidenced by their presence here today, have come to realize that their destiny is tied up with our destiny. [*Applause*] And they have come to realize that their freedom is inextricably bound to our freedom. We cannot walk alone.

And as we walk, we must make the pledge that we shall always march ahead. We cannot turn back. There are those who are asking the devotees of civil rights, "When will you be satisfied?" (*Never*)

We can never be satisfied as long as the Negro is the victim of the unspeakable horrors of police brutality. We can never be satisfied [*Applause*] as long as our bodies, heavy with the fatigue of travel, cannot gain lodging in the motels of the highways and the hotels of the cities. [*Applause*] We cannot be satisfied as long as the Negro's basic mobility is from a smaller ghetto to a larger one. We can never be satisfied as long as our children are stripped of their selfhood and robbed of their dignity by signs stating "for whites only." [*Applause*] We cannot be satisfied as long as a Negro in Mississippi cannot vote and a Negro in New York believes he has nothing for which to vote. (*Yes*) [*Applause*] No, no, we are not satisfied and we will not be satisfied until justice rolls down like waters and righteousness like a mighty stream. [*Applause*]

I am not unmindful that some of you have come here out of great trials and tribulations. (*My Lord*) Some of you have come fresh from narrow jail cells. Some of you have come from areas where your quest for freedom left you battered by the storms of persecution (*Yes*) and staggered by the winds of police brutality. You have been the veterans of creative suffering. Continue to work with the faith that unearned suffering is redemptive. Go back to Mississippi (*Yes*), go back to Alabama, go back to South Carolina, go back to Georgia, go back to Louisiana, go back to the slums and ghettos of our northern cities, knowing that somehow this situation can and will be changed. (*Yes*) Let us not wallow in the valley of despair.

I say to you today, my friends [*Applause*], so even though we face the difficulties of today and tomorrow, I still have a dream. (*Yes*) It is a dream deeply rooted in the American dream.

I have a dream that one day (*Yes*) this nation will rise up and live out the true meaning of its creed: "We hold these truths to be self-evident, that all men are created equal." (*Yes*) [*Applause*]

I have a dream that one day on the red hills of Georgia, the sons of former slaves and the sons of former slave owners will be able to sit down together at the table of brotherhood.

I have a dream that one day even the state of Mississippi, a state sweltering with the heat of injustice (*Well*), sweltering with the heat of oppression, will be transformed into an oasis of freedom and justice.

I have a dream (*Well*) [*Applause*] that my four little children will one day live in a nation where they will not be judged by the color of their skin but by the content of their character. (*My Lord*) I have a dream today. [*Applause*]

I have a dream that one day down in Alabama, with its vicious racists, with its governor having his lips dripping with the words of "interposition" and "nullification" (*Yes*), one day right there in Alabama little black boys and black girls will be able to join hands with little white boys and white girls as sisters and brothers. I have a dream today. [*Applause*]

I have a dream that one day every valley shall be exalted (*Yes*), and every hill and mountain shall be made low; the rough places will be made plain, and the crooked places will be made straight (*Yes*); and the glory of the Lord shall be revealed, and all flesh shall see it together. (*Yes*)

This is our hope. This is the faith that I go back to the South with. (*Yes*) With this faith we will be able to hew out of the mountain of despair a stone of hope. (*Yes*) With this faith we will be able to transform the jangling discords of our nation into a beautiful symphony of brotherhood. (*Talk about it*) With this faith (*My Lord*) we will be able to work together, to pray together, to struggle together, to go to jail together, to stand up for freedom together, knowing that we will be free one day. [*Applause*] This will be the day [*Applause continues*], this will be the day when all of God's children (*Yes*) will be able to sing with new meaning:

My country, 'tis of thee (*Yes*), sweet land of liberty, of thee I sing.
Land where my fathers died, land of the pilgrim's pride (*Yes*),
From every mountainside, let freedom ring!

And if America is to be a great nation, this must become true.

And so let freedom ring (*Yes*) from the prodigious hilltops of New Hampshire.

Let freedom ring from the mighty mountains of New York.

Let freedom ring from the heightening Alleghenies of Pennsylvania. (*Yes, That's right*)

Let freedom ring from the snowcapped Rockies of Colorado. (*Well*)

Let freedom ring from the curvaceous slopes of California. (*Yes*)

But not only that: Let freedom ring from Stone Mountain of Georgia. (*Yes*)

Let freedom ring from Lookout Mountain of Tennessee. (*Yes*)

Let freedom ring from every hill and molehill of Mississippi. (*Yes*)

From every mountainside, let freedom ring. [*Applause*]

And when this happens [*Applause continues*], when we allow freedom ring, when we let it ring from every village and every hamlet, from every state and every city (*Yes*), we will be able to speed up that day when all of God's children, black men and white men, Jews and Gentiles, Protestants and Catholics, will be able to join hands and sing in the words of the old Negro spiritual:

Free at last! (*Yes*) Free at last!
Thank God Almighty, we are free at last! [*Applause*]

DELIVERED AT THE MARCH ON WASHINGTON
FOR JOBS AND FREEDOM,
WASHINGTON, D.C., 28 AUGUST 1963.

EULOGY FOR THE YOUNG VICTIMS OF THE SIXTEENTH STREET BAPTIST CHURCH BOMBING

INTRODUCTION BY REVEREND FRED SHUTTLESWORTH

 t was in Birmingham in 1954 that I first met Dr. Martin Luther King, Jr., while the city buzzed and chatted about the "young man with a Ph.D." In a short meeting with him, I, the "young agitator," was quite impressed with his unassuming disposition, his humility, and his heartfelt belief in nonviolent direct action to end segregation in the South.

Being preachers, we knew segregation was wrong; God's word teaches nonviolence, and Gandhi's example of suffering and victory in India led us to believe that nonviolent action was the way to achieve freedom. The 1954 Supreme Court decision against school segregation gave us new hope, and we firmly sensed that the tide of American injustice was beginning to turn. Despite southern reactions to the decision—attempts at interposition and nullification, citizens' councils, segregated officials and judiciary, police terror, the Ku Klux Klan—we Negro leaders kept contact, cooperating and preparing plans to overthrow segregation, first by nonviolent appeals to conscience, and then by nonviolent direct action.

In retaliation, Alabama outlawed the NAACP in June 1956, loosing a series of bombings, beatings, and harassment of defenseless Negroes. But less than two weeks later, the Alabama Christian Movement for Human Rights (ACMHR) was founded under my direction, challenging all aspects of segregation in Bull Connor's Birmingham. The ACMHR suffered untold indignities for seven years before combining with Dr. King's SCLC, thus launching the massive nonviolent demonstrations of 1963—demonstrations that literally broke the back of legal segregation in the South.

An exceptional man in such violent times, Dr. King truly practiced what he preached. *He lived a nonviolent life.* He was disturbed to wound another person's spirit, even while speaking the truth in sometimes contentious staff and board meetings. Once, in Montgomery, I saw a man strike him, and he did not grimace or show anger. Instead, he turned a melancholy, forgiving face to his young white assailant, and refused to prosecute. During the Mississippi Meredith March, a Klansman with a full gun rack in his truck nearly ran us down, stopping within five feet of Martin and me. Martin did not try to jump out of the way; he only said resignedly, "Well, if this is where God wants it, we'll just have to go home from here."

It was also during that march that he kept his remarkably stoic calm as Stokely Carmichael frequently interrupted him with cries of "Black Power."

His calm aura translated into a refreshingly informal attitude, as well. Once, while lecturing young President Kennedy by phone on the necessity of nonviolent "creative tension," he paused mid-sentence to say, "Wait a minute, Mr. President. Ralph, bring me a couple pieces of chicken, please, and bring some more of that bread! Fred, ain't this some great bread?"

We believed in nonviolence, yes, and it did work— we marched, we sat in, we campaigned. Victory came only when thousands of children and adults—with fervor and enthusiasm—endured fire hoses, dog bites, police brutality, and inhumane treatment. We kept the jails full, the courts clogged, and brought shopping to a standstill. We stopped *cities*. We emerged victorious many times. Still, there is always a moment when one stops and asks: *At what price did this victory come?*

The Klan bombing of the Sixteenth Street Baptist Church that killed four beautiful, innocent girls at worship brought heartache and sorrow to their families, gloom to Birmingham, and recognition of true brutality to the nation. My heart ached with pain as we searched for answers. I thought of the thousands of children who marched in the face of death. I thought of my own, and my family's, brushes with death. Would the grieving parents and friends of these four girls entertain thoughts of anger and blame, or would they accept their great loss as God's will?

Solomon reasoned that *God hath put eternity in*

man's heart. Dr. King's eulogy portrays these four innocents as entering life only briefly, playing nobly and well their parts on the stage of history, and then moving through the curtain back into eternity. The sermon weaves from their deaths a fabric of messages aimed at those who *should* be active and vocal in the crusade for freedom and dignity: the silent minister, the vacillating politician, the compromising federal government, and the Negro who accepts segregation without challenge. The courage to listen and act upon Dr. King's message—courage, not caution—can change a system that causes the death of children:

> The wrath of man shall be praising Thee,
> for God will bring good from this evil act
> of murder, allowing the blood of the innocents to be a redemptive force for the city
> and Southland. The Prophet reminds that
> bitterness and thoughts of retaliation would
> not be helpful; but love can be redeeming
> to any person, even of the lowest mind.

Dr. King's words to the grieving families point out the only true democracy: the inevitable death of every person, regardless of status or color. He lifted them with Christianity's assurance that the resurrection has taken death's sting and power, so death is not an end, but an open door to eternal life.

Finally, Dr. King's eulogy for these martyred children does not dwell on the future glory and happiness of Heaven. Rather, it remains an eloquent and loving appeal to conscience for personal and active commitment to make and live earthly life better: to defend justice, human dignity, and the worth of all human beings. The God of Heaven gave us this life on earth to live and to love. Heaven begins now for those who strive to make this life better.

FRED SHUTTLESWORTH spearheaded the decade-long movement to end segregation in Birmingham, Alabama, and co-founded the Southern Christian Leadership Conference with Dr. King. A national civil rights leader and preacher, he now serves on the advisory board for the Congress of Racial Equality and as pastor of Greater New Light Baptist Church in Cincinnati, Ohio.

EULOGY FOR THE YOUNG VICTIMS OF THE SIXTEENTH STREET BAPTIST CHURCH BOMBING

This afternoon we gather in the quiet of this sanctuary to pay our last tribute of respect to these beautiful children of God.* They entered the stage of history just a few years ago, and in the brief years that they were privileged to act on this mortal stage, they played their parts exceedingly well. Now the curtain falls; they move through the exit; the drama of their earthly life comes to a close. They are now committed back to that eternity from which they came.†

These children—unoffending, innocent, and beautiful—were the victims of one of the most vicious and tragic crimes ever perpetrated against humanity. And yet they died nobly. They are the martyred heroines of a holy crusade for freedom and human dignity.

---

*This eulogy was delivered at the funeral service for three of the children—Addie Mae Collins, Carol Denise McNair, and Cynthia Diane Wesley—killed in the bombing. A separate service was held for the fourth victim, Carole Robertson.

†This introductory paragraph is not included in the known recording of the "Eulogy," which was edited for radio broadcast but is preserved in print at the Martin Luther King, Jr., Center for Nonviolent Social Change in Atlanta, Georgia.

And so this afternoon in a real sense they have something to say to each of us in their death. They have something to say to every minister of the gospel who has remained silent behind the safe security of stained-glass windows. They have something to say to every politician [*Audience:*] (*Yeah*) who has fed his constituents with the stale bread of hatred and the spoiled meat of racism. They have something to say to a federal government that has compromised with the undemocratic practices of southern Dixiecrats (*Yeah*) and the blatant hypocrisy of right-wing northern Republicans. (*Speak*) They have something to say to every Negro (*Yeah*) who has passively accepted the evil system of segregation and who has stood on the sidelines in a mighty struggle for justice. They say to each of us, black and white alike, that we must substitute courage for caution. They say to us that we must be concerned not merely about who murdered them, but about the system, the way of life, the philosophy which produced the murderers. Their death says to us that we must work passionately and unrelentingly for the realization of the American dream.

And so my friends, they did not die in vain. (*Yeah*) God still has a way of wringing good out of evil. (*Oh yes*) And history has proven over and over again that unmerited suffering is redemptive. The innocent blood of these little girls may well serve as a redemptive force (*Yeah*) that will bring new light to this dark city. (*Yeah*) The holy Scripture says, "A little child shall lead them." (*Oh yeah*) The death of these little children may lead our whole Southland (*Yeah*) from the low road of man's inhumanity to man to the high road of peace and brotherhood. (*Yes*) These tragic deaths may lead our nation to substitute an aristocracy of character for an aristocracy of color. The spilled blood of these innocent girls may cause the whole citizenry of Birmingham (*Yeah*) to transform the negative extremes of a dark past into the positive extremes of a bright future. Indeed this tragic event may cause the white South to come to terms with its conscience.

And so I stand here to say this afternoon to all assembled here, that in spite of the darkness of this hour (*Well*), we must not despair. (*Well*) We must not become bitter (*That's right*), nor must we harbor the desire to retaliate with violence. No, we must not lose faith in our white brothers. (*Yes*) Somehow we must believe that the most misguided among them can learn to respect the dignity and the worth of all human personality.

May I now say a word to you, the members of the bereaved families? It is almost impossible to say anything that can console you at this difficult hour and remove the deep clouds of disappointment which are floating in your mental skies. But I hope you can find a little consolation from the universality of this experience. Death comes to every individual. There is an amazing democracy about death. It is not aristocracy for some of the people, but a democracy for all of the people. Kings die and beggars die; rich men and poor men die; old people die and young people die. Death comes to the innocent and it comes to the guilty. Death is the irreducible common denominator of all men.

I hope you can find some consolation from Christianity's affirmation that death is not the end. Death is not a period that ends the great sentence of life, but a comma that punctuates it to more lofty significance. Death is not a blind alley that leads the human race into a state of nothingness, but an open door which leads man into life eternal. Let this daring faith, this great invincible surmise, be your sustaining power during these trying days.*

Now I say to you in conclusion, life is hard, at times as hard as crucible steel. It has its bleak and difficult moments. Like the ever-flowing waters of the river, life has its moments of drought and its moments of flood. (*Yes*) Like the ever-changing cycle of the seasons, life has the soothing warmth of its summers and the piercing chill of its winters. (*Yeah*) And if one will hold on, he will discover that God walks with him (*Well*), and that God is able (*Yes*) to lift you from the fatigue of despair to the buoyancy of hope, and transform dark and desolate valleys into sunlit paths of inner peace.

And so today, you do not walk alone. You gave to this world wonderful children. They didn't live long lives, but they lived meaningful lives. (*Well*) Their lives were distressingly small in quantity, but glowingly large in quality. (*Yeah*) And no greater tribute can be paid to you as parents, and no greater epitaph can come to them as children, than where they died and what they were doing when they died. (*Yeah*) They did not die in the dives and dens of Birming-

---

*The two preceding paragraphs, like King's introductory statements, are preserved in print but not in the extant recording.

ham (*Well*), nor did they die discussing and listening to filthy jokes. (*Yeah*) They died between the sacred walls of the church of God (*Yes*), and they were discussing the eternal meaning (*Yes*) of love. This stands out as a beautiful, beautiful thing for all generations. (*Yes*) Shakespeare had Horatio to say some beautiful words as he stood over the dead body of Hamlet. And today as I stand over the remains of these beautiful, darling girls, I paraphrase the words of Shakespeare (*Well*): Good night, sweet princesses. Good night, those who symbolize a new day. (*Yes*) And may the flight of angels (*That's right*) take thee to thy eternal rest. God bless you.

DELIVERED AT SIXTH AVENUE BAPTIST CHURCH,
BIRMINGHAM, ALABAMA,
18 SEPTEMBER 1963.

ACCEPTANCE ADDRESS FOR THE NOBEL PEACE PRIZE

INTRODUCTION BY HIS HOLINESS THE DALAI LAMA

I t was entirely fitting that Dr. Martin Luther King, Jr., should have been a recipient of the Nobel Peace Prize, for he is one of the great heroes of our time. When his people were crying out for freedom, he had the courage to lead them to it. What made him great was his determination that others should not be harmed in the struggle. When he said, "Freedom is not given, it is won," many people would have taken it as a cue to take up arms. Dr. King taught instead that people should stand up for themselves, but with love and understanding for those who stood against them. He recognized that our enemies can be our greatest teachers.

As Dr. King said, nonviolence is power, but it is the right and good use of power. This is because it is related to the power of truth. People do not like to be bullied, cheated, or lied to by either an individual or a system. Such acts are contrary to the essential human spirit. Truth is the best guarantor of freedom and democracy. It does not matter whether you are weak or strong, or whether your cause has many or few adherents. Truth will still prevail.

Despite their quite different backgrounds, Dr. King has joined Mahatma Gandhi as a continuing beacon of inspiration to further peaceful revolutions in recent years that, in turn, offer future generations a wonderful example of successful, nonviolent change. What both these great men affirmed is that the desire for both peace and freedom lies at the most fundamental level of human nature and that violence is its complete antithesis.

It is an honor for me to contribute my remarks to this publication of Dr. King's Nobel Peace Prize acceptance speech. I was a young man when he delivered it, newly exiled from my homeland and but dimly acquainted with the world at large. However, my own experience has given me deep understanding of the pressures and sorrows he bore in maintaining his adherence to nonviolence. Today, after more than forty years of Chinese occupation, the circumstances of my people in Tibet is very like that of the African-Americans for whom Dr. King struggled. They have become an oppressed minority in their own land. Therefore, recalling his great work for civil rights in America, I appeal to those who read this to extend the same concern, not only for Tibetans, but for everyone deprived of their fundamental human rights throughout the world.

HIS HOLINESS THE FOURTEENTH DALAI LAMA is the exiled spiritual leader of Tibetan Buddhists and winner of the 1989 Nobel Peace Prize for his efforts to achieve social change through nonviolent protest.

Acceptance Address
for the
Nobel Peace Prize

Your Majesty, Your Royal Highness, Mr. President, excellencies, ladies and gentlemen: I accept the Nobel Prize for Peace at a moment when twenty-two million Negroes of the United States are engaged in a creative battle to end the long night of racial injustice. I accept this award on behalf of a civil rights movement which is moving with determination and a majestic scorn for risk and danger to establish a reign of freedom and a rule of justice.

I am mindful that only yesterday in Birmingham, Alabama, our children, crying out for brotherhood, were answered with fire hoses, snarling dogs, and even death. I am mindful that only yesterday in Philadelphia, Mississippi, young people seeking to secure the right to vote were brutalized and murdered. I am mindful that debilitating and grinding poverty afflicts my people and chains them to the lowest rung of the economic ladder.

Therefore, I must ask why this prize is awarded to a movement which is beleaguered and committed to unrelenting struggle, and to a movement which has not yet won the very peace and brotherhood which is the essence of the Nobel Prize. After contemplation, I conclude that this award, which I receive on behalf of that movement, is a profound recognition that nonviolence is the answer to the crucial political and moral questions of our time: the need for man to overcome oppression and violence without resorting to violence and oppression.

Civilization and violence are antithetical concepts. Negroes of the United States, following the people of India, have demonstrated that nonviolence is not sterile passivity, but a powerful moral force which makes for social transformation. Sooner or later, all the peoples of the world will have to discover a way to live together in peace, and thereby transform this pending cosmic elegy into a creative psalm of brotherhood. If this is to be achieved, man must evolve for all human conflict a method which rejects revenge, aggression, and retaliation. The foundation of such a method is love.

The torturous road which has led from Montgomery, Alabama, to Oslo bears witness to this truth, and this is a road over which millions of Negroes are traveling to find a new sense of dignity. This same road has opened for all Americans a new era of progress and hope. It has led to a new civil rights bill, and it will, I am convinced, be widened and lengthened into a superhighway of justice as Negro and white men in increasing numbers create alliances to overcome their common problems.

I accept this award today with an abiding faith in America and an audacious faith in the future of mankind. I refuse to accept despair as the final response to the ambiguities of history.

I refuse to accept the idea that the "is–ness" of man's present nature makes him morally incapable of reaching up for the eternal "ought–ness" that forever confronts him.

I refuse to accept the idea that man is mere flotsam and jetsam in the river of life, unable to influence the unfolding events which surround him.

I refuse to accept the view that mankind is so tragically bound to the starless midnight of racism and war that the bright daybreak of peace and brotherhood can never become a reality.

I refuse to accept the cynical notion that nation after nation must spiral down a militaristic stairway into the hell of nuclear annihilation.

I believe that unarmed truth and unconditional love will have the final word in reality. This is why right, temporarily defeated, is stronger than evil triumphant.

I believe that even amid today's mortar bursts and whining bullets, there is still hope for a brighter tomorrow.

I believe that wounded justice, lying prostrate on the blood-flowing streets of our nations, can be lifted from this dust of shame to reign supreme among the children of men.

I have the audacity to believe that peoples everywhere can have three meals a day for their bodies, education and culture for their minds, and dignity, equality, and freedom for their spirits.

I believe that what self-centered men have torn down, men other-centered can build up.

I still believe that one day mankind will bow before the altars of God and be crowned triumphant over war and bloodshed, and nonviolent redemptive goodwill proclaimed the rule of the land. And the lion and the lamb shall lie down together, and every man shall sit under his own vine and fig tree, and none shall be afraid.

I still believe that we shall overcome.

This faith can give us courage to face the uncertainties of the future. It will give our tired feet new strength as we continue our forward stride toward the city of freedom. When our days become dreary with low-hovering clouds and our nights become darker than a thousand midnights, we will know that we are living in the creative turmoil of a genuine civilization struggling to be born.

Today I come to Oslo as a trustee, inspired and with renewed dedication to humanity. I accept this prize on behalf of all men who love peace and brotherhood. I say I come as a trustee, for in the depths of my heart I am aware that this prize is much more than an honor to me personally. Every time I take a flight I am always mindful of the many people who make a successful journey possible, the known pilots and the unknown ground crew. You honor the dedicated pilots of our struggle, who have sat at the controls as the freedom movement soared into orbit. You honor, once again, Chief Lutuli of South Africa, whose struggles with and for his people are still met with the most brutal expression of man's inhumanity to man. You honor the ground crew, without whose labor and sacrifice the jet flights to freedom could never have left the earth. Most of these people will never make the headlines, and their names will never appear in *Who's Who.* Yet, when years have rolled past and when the blazing light of truth is focused on this marvelous age in which we live, men and women will know and children will be taught that we have a finer land, a better people, a more noble civilization because these humble children of God were willing to suffer for righteousness' sake.

I think Alfred Nobel would know what I mean when I say I accept this award in the spirit of a curator of some precious heirloom which he holds in trust for its true owners: all those to whom truth is beauty, and beauty, truth, and in whose eyes the beauty of genuine brotherhood and peace is more precious than diamonds or silver or gold. Thank you. [*Applause*]

DELIVERED IN OSLO, NORWAY,
10 DECEMBER 1964.

Address at the
Conclusion of the
Selma to
Montgomery
March

INTRODUCTION BY REPRESENTATIVE JOHN LEWIS

r. Martin Luther King, Jr., was my friend, my brother, my inspiration, and my colleague. I first met Dr. King when I was eighteen years old, in 1958. I wrote a letter seeking his advice because I wanted to attend Troy State University, an all-white state college near my home in Troy, Alabama. A short while later, I received a round-trip bus ticket from Dr. King. He wanted to meet me and discuss my plans to desegregate Troy State. I took the trip to Montgomery without knowing that the trip would change my life. From that first meeting to the day of his death in Memphis in 1968, I was inspired by the life and prophetic vision of Dr. King.

Dr. King was perhaps one of the most gifted orators of our time. This man—this son of the American South, this citizen of the world—had the ability to produce light in dark places. He had the capacity to bring hope in a time of hopelessness. When he spoke, the masses knew from his words that they were somebody. When Dr. King called upon us to march, we marched knowing that truth was on our side. No matter where he spoke, an electricity filled the air. After listening to Dr. King we were so inspired and so moved, we were prepared to march into Hell's fires. Like all great orators, Dr. King was keenly aware of the audience. His dramatic cadence and voice was like a baby's lullaby; you could not resist his call to your conscience.

This speech is historically significant in the canon of powerful, emotion-charged speeches by Dr. King. It took place after weeks and months of fighting for the right to vote in Selma, Alabama. In the heart of the Black Belt of Alabama only 2 percent of African-Americans were registered to vote. Some had been arrested, jailed, beaten, and even killed for encouraging others to register to vote. Some had been evicted from their homes and fired from their jobs because they dared to register to vote.

The whole drive for the right to vote came to a head on March 7, 1965.

About six hundred of us—mostly elderly black men and women and a few young people—tried to dramatize to the nation and to the world that we wanted to become participants in the democratic process. Crossing the Alabama River over the Edmund Pettus Bridge in Selma, we were brutally attacked by members of the Alabama State Troopers. They came beating us with bullwhips and nightsticks. They trampled us with horses. That Sunday became known as "Bloody Sunday."

Dr. King came to Selma the next day as he had done so many times before. He issued a nationwide appeal for religious leaders to come to Selma and to walk the same path we had taken on Bloody Sunday. More than a thousand priests, rabbis, nuns, and ministers responded to the Macedonian call of Dr. King. They lined up early on Tuesday, March 9, after attending a religious service in Brown Chapel AME Church. They quietly and orderly walked through the streets of Selma and crossed the Edmund Pettus Bridge. When they came to the same point where we were beaten on Bloody Sunday, the marchers knelt and prayed. Facing again a sea of state troopers, the marchers turned back and awaited a court order allowing us to march from Selma to Montgomery.

I will never forget as long as I live when more than ten thousand of us began our march from Selma to Montgomery two weeks later on a Sunday afternoon, March 21. The march led that day by Dr. King was like Gandhi's march to the sea. There was something so peaceful, so holy, so profoundly spiritual about the moving feet on the pavement. As we marched with Dr. King, it seemed liked the Heavenly Host was walking with us. We sang. We prayed. One day the rain came down. The skies opened up. The rain could not stop us. We were not afraid. We truly were, as the Negro spiritual goes, "wadin' in the water." We were God's children, wadin' in the water.

We had been warned that we would never make it from Selma to Montgomery.

When we made it across the Alabama River into the city of Montgomery, it was almost like crossing our own Red Sea, our own River of Jordan. We made it to the steps of the state capitol on Thursday, March 25, 1965, and yet people said we would never get there. We weren't supposed to be there. Dr. King put it best in this address: "Our feet are tired, but our souls are rested." Indeed, our souls were rested that afternoon because the march from Selma to Montgomery was a shining moment in human history. People from every corner of our nation came on the march and they spoke against the customs and laws of the South with their weary feet. Dr. King once said, "nothing could stop the marching feet of a determined people." That day, on the steps of the Alabama state capitol, we dramatized our determination to change America forever.

In this setting, Dr. King gave this moving, powerful address. He tells the world that we have marched and that we continue to march because "truth is marching on." From his first words to his last sentence, we are told that thousands participated in a mighty walk from Selma, Alabama.

Reading this address today brings to mind a vivid image of marching feet. It was so fitting and so moving for our march to end in Montgomery because this was where Dr. King started preaching his philosophy and discipline of nonviolence. And the march from Selma to Montgomery was the last of the great nonviolent protests. It was one of the finest moments of the movement. When Dr. King gave this address on that Thursday afternoon, he spoke from his heart and the depths of his soul. He spoke for all of us. Dr. King called upon the conscience of the nation.

In this moving and eloquent address, Dr. King urged us to march on. He pleaded with sheer poetry: "Remain committed to nonviolence. Our aim must never be to defeat or humiliate the white man, but to win his friendship and understanding. We must come to see that the end we seek is a society at peace with itself, a society that can live with its conscience. And that will be a day not of the white man, not of the black man. That will be the day of man as man." I draw from these words a message of hope: We must never, ever give up. We must use our bodies, use our hands, use our feet, and use our voices as tools to help build the Beloved Community.

This march was like Moses leading the children of Israel out of Egypt. Dr. King was leading African-Americans and the whole nation out of political slavery into full political participation. This protest and the message of this address helped open up the political process for all Americans. Dr. King must be looked upon not just as one of the founding fathers of the New America, but as a twentieth-century prophet. He predicted, he prophesied, and he prayed that we would come to the point where we would lay down the burden of race and create one community, one family, the American family. I can still hear his voice and recall with crystal clarity the call to my soul when Dr. King asked: "When will the radiant star of hope be plunged against the nocturnal bosom of this lonely night, plucked from weary souls with chains of fear and the manacles of death? . . . How long? Not long, because the arc of the moral universe is long, but it bends toward justice." Yes, this is poetry, but it is also an enduring call to my soul and the souls of so many who fell under the spell of Dr. King's oratory.

As I read this address in a different time and a different place in history, I am moved by its enduring power to stir our conscience. His spirit, his ideas, his philosophy, his truth march on in this address. This address could be called "We Keep Marching On." I say this because there is no road map, no blueprint, no simple four-lane highway, no jet stream in the sky for the arc bending toward justice, toward the dream of a Beloved Community. Dr. King tells us that we must be creative; we must find a way and keep marching on.

Every phrase is touched with poetic beauty. His words could lift your spirit. Sometimes you felt you were riding on the wings of angels. This address survives to this day because of its timeless vision of a better and more peaceful world.

Starting with the imagery of weary feet, Dr. King reminds us that we must find a way to do the work of the Master. Today, in our time, we have the power to bring down the walls of racism, the walls of poverty, and the walls of intolerance. With each of us inspired by the message of this address and the gifts of the orator, we march on. And we march on with faith and hope and love.

* * *

JOHN LEWIS was a student leader of the Nashville sit-in movement, and a cofounder and later chairman of the Student Nonviolent Coordinating Committee. Lewis spoke at the August 28, 1963, March on Washington for Jobs and Freedom, and led the March 7, 1965, Bloody Sunday march in Selma, Alabama. Under his direction, the Voter Education Project added over four million minorities to the voter rolls. Lewis was elected to the United States Congress in 1986, a position he continues to hold.

ADDRESS AT THE CONCLUSION OF THE SELMA TO MONTGOMERY MARCH

My dear and abiding friend, Ralph Abernathy, and to all of the distinguished Americans seated here on the rostrum, my friends and coworkers of the state of Alabama, and to all of the freedom-loving people who have assembled here this afternoon from all over our nation and from all over the world: Last Sunday, more than eight thousand of us started on a mighty walk from Selma, Alabama. We have walked through desolate valleys and across the trying hills. We have walked on meandering highways and rested our bodies on rocky byways. Some of our faces are burned from the outpourings of the sweltering sun. Some have literally slept in the mud. We have been drenched by the rain. [*Audience:*] (*Speak*) Our bodies are tired, our feet are somewhat sore.

But today, as I stand before you and think back over that great march, I can say, as Sister Pollard said— a seventy-year-old Negro woman who lived in this community during the bus boycott—and one day, she was asked while walking if she didn't want to ride. And when she answered, "No," the person said, "Well, aren't you tired?" With her ungrammatical profundity,

she said, "My feets is tired, but my soul is rested."
(*Yes sir, All right*) And in a real sense this afternoon,
we can say that our feet are tired (*Yes sir*), but our
souls are rested.

They told us we wouldn't get here. There were those
who said that we would get here only over their dead
bodies (*Well, Yes sir, Talk*), but all the world today
knows that we are here and we are standing before
the forces of power in the state of Alabama saying,
"We ain't goin' let nobody turn us around." (*Yes sir,
Speak*) [*Applause*]

Now it is not an accident that one of the great
marches of American history should terminate in
Montgomery, Alabama. (*Yes sir*) Just ten years ago, in
this very city, a new philosophy was born of the Negro
struggle. Montgomery was the first city in the South
in which the entire Negro community united and
squarely faced its age-old oppressors. (*Yes sir, Well*)
Out of this struggle, more than bus [*de*]segregation
was won; a new idea, more powerful than guns or
clubs, was born. Negroes took it and carried it across
the South in epic battles (*Yes sir, Speak*) that electri-
fied the nation (*Well*) and the world.

Yet, strangely, the climactic conflicts always were
fought and won on Alabama soil. After Montgomery's,
heroic confrontations loomed up in Mississippi,
Arkansas, Georgia, and elsewhere. But not until the
colossus of segregation was challenged in Birmingham
did the conscience of America begin to bleed. White
America was profoundly aroused by Birmingham because it witnessed the whole community of Negroes
facing terror and brutality with majestic scorn and

heroic courage. And from the wells of this democratic spirit, the nation finally forced Congress (*Well*) to write legislation (*Yes sir*), in the hope that it would eradicate the stain of Birmingham. The Civil Rights Act of 1964 gave Negroes some part of their rightful dignity (*Speak sir*), but without the vote it was dignity without strength. (*Yes sir*)

Once more the method of nonviolent resistance (*Yes*) was unsheathed from its scabbard, and once again an entire community was mobilized to confront the adversary. (*Yes sir*) And again the brutality of a dying order shrieks across the land. Yet Selma, Alabama, became a shining moment in the conscience of man. If the worst in American life lurked in its dark streets, the best of American instincts arose passionately from across the nation to overcome it. (*Yes sir, Speak*) There never was a moment in American history (*Yes sir*) more honorable and more inspiring than the pilgrimage of clergymen and laymen of every race and faith pouring into Selma to face danger (*Yes*) at the side of its embattled Negroes.

The confrontation of good and evil compressed in the tiny community of Selma (*Speak, Speak*) generated the massive power (*Yes sir, Yes sir*) to turn the whole nation to a new course. A president born in the South (*Well*) had the sensitivity to feel the will of the country (*Speak sir*), and in an address that will live in history as one of the most passionate pleas for human rights ever made by a president of our nation, he pledged the might of the federal government to cast off the centuries-old blight. President Johnson rightly praised the courage of the Negro for awakening the conscience of the nation. (*Yes sir*)

On our part we must pay our profound respect to the white Americans who cherish their democratic traditions over the ugly customs and privileges of generations and come forth boldly to join hands with us. (*Yes sir*) From Montgomery to Birmingham (*Yes sir*), from Birmingham to Selma (*Yes sir*), from Selma back to Montgomery (*Yes*), a trail wound in a circle long and often bloody, yet it has become a highway up from darkness. (*Yes sir*) Alabama has tried to nurture and defend evil, but evil is choking to death in the dusty roads and streets of this state. (*Yes sir, Speak sir*) So I stand before you this afternoon (*Speak sir, Well*) with the conviction that segregation is on its deathbed in Alabama, and the only thing uncertain about it is how costly the segregationists and Wallace will make the funeral. (*Go ahead, Yes sir*) [*Applause*]

Our whole campaign in Alabama has been centered around the right to vote. In focusing the attention of the nation and the world today on the flagrant denial of the right to vote, we are exposing the very origin, the root cause, of racial segregation in the Southland. Racial segregation as a way of life did not come about as a natural result of hatred between the races immediately after the Civil War. There were no laws segregating the races then. As the noted historian C. Vann Woodward, in his book *The Strange Career of Jim Crow*, clearly points out, the segregation of the races was really a political stratagem employed by the emerging Bourbon interests in the South to keep the southern masses divided and southern labor the cheapest in the land. You see, it was a simple thing to keep the poor white masses working for near-starvation wages in the years that followed the Civil War. Why, if the poor white plantation or mill worker became dissatisfied with his low wages, the plantation or mill owner would merely threaten to fire him and hire a former Negro slave and pay him even less. Thus, the southern wage level was kept almost unbearably low.

Toward the end of the Reconstruction era, something very significant happened. (*Listen to him*) There developed what was known as the Populist Movement. (*Speak sir*) The leaders of this movement began awakening the poor white masses (*Yes sir*) and the former Negro slaves to the fact that they were being fleeced by the emerging Bourbon interests. Not only that, but they began uniting the Negro and white masses (*Yeah*) into a voting bloc that threatened to drive the Bourbon interests from the command posts of political power in the South.

To meet this threat, the southern aristocracy began immediately to engineer this development of a segregated society. (*Right*) I want you to follow me through here because this is very important to see the roots of racism and the denial of the right to vote. Through their control of mass media, they revised the doctrine of white supremacy. They saturated the thinking of the poor white masses with it (*Yes*), thus clouding their minds to the real issue involved in the Populist Movement. They then directed the placement on the books of the South of laws that made it a crime for Negroes and whites to come together as equals at any level. (*Yes sir*) And that did it. That crippled and eventually destroyed the Populist Movement of the nineteenth century.

If it may be said of the slavery era that the white man took the world and gave the Negro Jesus, then it may be said of the Reconstruction era that the southern aristocracy took the world and gave the poor white man Jim Crow. (*Yes sir*) He gave him Jim Crow, and when his wrinkled stomach cried out for the food that his empty pockets could not provide (*Yes sir*), he ate Jim Crow, a psychological bird that told him that no matter how bad off he was, at least he was a white man, better than the black man. (*Right sir*) And he ate Jim Crow. And when his undernourished children cried out for the necessities that his low wages could not provide, he showed them the Jim Crow signs on the buses and in the stores, on the streets and in the public buildings. (*Yes sir*) And his children, too, learned to feed upon Jim Crow (*Speak*), their last outpost of psychological oblivion. (*Yes sir*)

Thus the threat of the free exercise of the ballot by the Negro and white masses alike resulted in the establishment of a segregated society. They segregated southern money from the poor whites; they segregated southern mores from the rich whites (*Yes sir*); they segregated southern churches from Christianity (*Yes sir*); they segregated southern minds from honest thinking (*Yes sir*); and they segregated the Negro from everything. (*Yes sir*) That's what happened when the Negro and white masses of the South threatened to unite and build a great society: a society of justice where none would prey upon the weakness of others, a society of plenty where greed and poverty would be done away, a society of brotherhood where every man would respect the dignity and worth of human personality. (*Yes sir*)

We've come a long way since that travesty of justice was perpetrated upon the American mind. James Weldon Johnson put it eloquently. He said:

We have come over a way
That with tears hath been watered. (*Yes sir*)
We have come treading our paths
Through the blood of the slaughtered. (*Yes sir*)

Out of the gloomy past (*Yes sir*),
Till now we stand at last
Where the white gleam
Of our bright star is cast. (*Speak sir*)

Today I want to tell the city of Selma (*Tell them, Doctor*), today I want to say to the state of Alabama (*Yes sir*), today I want to say to the people of America and the nations of the world, that we are not about to turn around. (*Yes sir*) We are on the move now. (*Yes sir*)

Yes, we are on the move and no wave of racism can stop us. (*Yes sir*) We are on the move now. The burning of our churches will not deter us. (*Yes sir*) The bombing of our homes will not dissuade us. (*Did you hear him, Yes sir*) We are on the move now. (*Yes sir*) The beating and killing of our clergymen and young people will not divert us. We are on the move now. (*Yes sir*) The wanton release of their known murderers will not discourage us. We are on the move now. (*Yes sir*) Like an idea whose time has come (*Yes sir*), not even the marching of mighty armies can halt us. (*Yes sir*) We are moving to the land of freedom. (*Yes sir*)

Let us therefore continue our triumphant march to the realization of the American dream. (*Yes sir*) Let us march on segregated housing (*Yes sir*) until every ghetto of social and economic depression dissolves, and Negroes and whites live side by side in decent, safe, and sanitary housing. (*Yes sir*) Let us march on segregated schools (*Let us march, Tell it*) until every vestige of segregated and inferior education becomes a thing of the past, and Negroes and whites study side by side in the socially healing context of the classroom.

Let us march on poverty (*Let us march*) until no American parent has to skip a meal so that their children may eat. (*Yes sir*) March on poverty (*Let us march*) until no starved man walks the streets of our cities and towns (*Yes sir*) in search of jobs that do not exist. (*Yes sir*) Let us march on poverty (*Let us march*) until wrinkled stomachs in Mississippi are filled (*That's right*), and the idle industries of Appalachia are realized and revitalized, and broken lives in sweltering ghettos are mended and remolded.

Let us march on ballot boxes (*Let's march*), march on ballot boxes until race-baiters disappear from the political arena. Let us march on ballot boxes until the salient misdeeds of bloodthirsty mobs (*Yes sir*) will be transformed into the calculated good deeds of orderly citizens. (*Speak, Doctor*) Let us march on ballot boxes

(*Let us march*) until the Wallaces of our nation tremble away in silence. Let us march on ballot boxes (*Let us march*) until we send to our city councils (*Yes sir*), state legislatures (*Yes sir*), and the United States Congress (*Yes sir*), men who will not fear to do justly, love mercy, and walk humbly with thy God.

Let us march on ballot boxes (*Let us march, March*) until brotherhood becomes more than a meaningless word in an opening prayer, but the order of the day on every legislative agenda. Let us march on ballot boxes (*Yes*) until all over Alabama God's children will be able to walk the earth in decency and honor.

There is nothing wrong with marching in this sense. (*Yes sir*) The Bible tells us that the mighty men of Joshua merely walked about the walled city of Jericho (*Yes*) and the barriers to freedom came tumbling down. (*Yes sir*) I like that old Negro spiritual (*Yes sir*) "Joshua Fit the Battle of Jericho." In its simple, yet colorful, depiction (*Yes sir*) of that great moment in biblical history, it tells us that:

Joshua fit the battle of Jericho (*Tell it*),
Joshua fit the battle of Jericho (*Yes sir*),
And the walls come tumbling down. (*Yes sir, Tell it*)

Up to the walls of Jericho they marched, spear in hand. (*Yes sir*)
"Go blow them ramhorns," Joshua cried,
" 'Cause the battle am in my hand." (*Yes sir*)

These words I have given you just as they were given us by their unknown, long-dead, dark-skinned originator. (*Yes sir*) Some now long-gone black bard bequeathed to posterity these words in ungrammatical form (*Yes sir*), yet with emphatic pertinence for all of us today.

The battle is in our hands. And we can answer with creative nonviolence the call to higher ground to which the new directions of our struggle summons us. (*Yes sir*) The road ahead is not altogether a smooth one. (*No*) There are no broad highways that lead us easily and inevitably to quick solutions. But we must keep going.

In the glow of the lamplight on my desk a few nights ago, I gazed again upon the wondrous sign of our times, full of hope and promise of the future. And I smiled to see in the newspaper photographs of many a decade ago, the faces so bright, so solemn, of our valiant heroes, the people of Montgomery. To this list may be added the names of all those (*Yes*) who have fought and, yes, died in the nonviolent army of our day: Medgar Evers (*Speak*); three civil rights workers in Mississippi last summer; William Moore, as has already been mentioned (*Yes sir*); the Reverend James Reeb (*Yes sir*); Jimmy Lee Jackson (*Yes sir*); and four little girls in the church of God in Birmingham on Sunday morning. (*Yes sir*) In spite of this, we must go on and be sure that they did not die in vain. (*Yes sir*) The pattern of their feet as they walked through Jim Crow barriers in the great stride toward freedom is the thunder of the marching men of Joshua (*Yes sir*), and the world rocks beneath their tread. (*Yes sir*)

My people, my people, listen. (*Yes sir*) The battle is in our hands. (*Yes sir*) The battle is in our hands in Mississippi and Alabama and all over the United States. (*Yes sir*) I know there is a cry today in Alabama, we see it in numerous editorials: "When will Martin Luther King, SCLC, SNCC, and all of these civil rights agitators and all of the white clergymen and labor leaders and students and others get out of our community and let Alabama return to normalcy?"

I have a message that I would like to leave with Alabama this evening. (*Tell it*) That is exactly what we don't want, and we will not allow it to happen (*Yes sir*), for we know that it was normalcy in Marion *(Yes sir)* that led to the brutal murder of Jimmy Lee Jackson. (*Speak*) It was normalcy in Birmingham (*Yes*) that led to the murder on Sunday morning of four beautiful, unoffending, innocent girls. It was normalcy on Highway 80 (*Yes sir*) that led state troopers to use tear gas and horses and billy clubs against unarmed human beings who were simply marching for justice. (*Speak sir*) It was normalcy by a café in Selma, Alabama, that led to the brutal beating of Reverend James Reeb.

It is normalcy all over our country (*Yes sir*) which leaves the Negro perishing on a lonely island of poverty in the midst of a vast ocean of material prosperity. It is normalcy all over Alabama (*Yeah*) that prevents the Negro from becoming a registered voter. (*Yes*) No, we will not allow Alabama (*Go ahead*) to return to normalcy. (*Yes sir*) [*Applause*]

The only normalcy that we will settle for (*Yes sir*) is the normalcy that recognizes the dignity and worth of all of God's children. The only normalcy that we will settle for is the normalcy that allows judgment to run down like waters, and righteousness like a mighty stream. (*Yes sir*) The only normalcy that we will settle for is the normalcy of brotherhood, the normalcy of true peace, the normalcy of justice.

And so as we go away this afternoon, let us go away more than ever before committed to this struggle and committed to nonviolence. I must admit to you there are still some difficult days ahead. We are still in for a season of suffering in many of the black belt counties of Alabama, many areas of Mississippi, many areas of Louisiana. I must admit to you there are still jail cells waiting for us, and dark and difficult moments. If we will go on with the faith that nonviolence and its power can transform dark yesterdays into bright tomorrows, we will be able to change all of these conditions.

And so I plead with you this afternoon as we go ahead: remain committed to nonviolence. Our aim must never be to defeat or humiliate the white man, but to win his friendship and understanding. We must come to see that the end we seek is a society at peace with itself, a society that can live with its conscience. And that will be a day not of the white man, not of the black man. That will be the day of man as man. (*Yes*)

I know you are asking today, "How long will it take?" (*Speak sir*) Somebody's asking, "How long will prejudice blind the visions of men, darken their understanding, and drive bright-eyed wisdom from her sacred throne?" Somebody's asking, "When will wounded justice, lying prostrate on the streets of Selma and Birmingham and communities all over the South, be lifted from this dust of shame to reign supreme among the children of men?" Somebody's asking, "When will the radiant star of hope be plunged against the nocturnal bosom of this lonely night (*Speak, Speak, Speak*), plucked from weary souls with chains of fear and the manacles of death? How long will justice be crucified (*Speak, Speak*), and truth bear it?" (*Yes sir*)

I come to say to you this afternoon, however difficult the moment (*Yes sir*), however frustrating the hour, it will not be long (*No sir*), because truth crushed to earth will rise again. (*Yes sir*)

How long? Not long (*Yes sir*), because no lie can live forever. (*Yes sir*)

How long? Not long (*All right, How long*), because you shall reap what you sow. (*Yes sir*)

How long? (*How long*) Not long. (*Not long*)

> Truth forever on the scaffold (*Speak*),
> Wrong forever on the throne (*Yes sir*),
> Yet that scaffold sways the future (*Yes sir*),
> And, behind the dim unknown,
> Standeth God within the shadow,
> Keeping watch above His own.

How long? Not long, because the arc of the moral universe is long, but it bends toward justice. (*Yes sir*)

How long? Not long (*Not long*), because:

Mine eyes have seen the glory of the coming of the Lord (*Yes sir*);

He is trampling out the vintage where the grapes of wrath are stored (*Yes*);
He has loosed the fateful lightning of his terrible swift sword (*Yes sir*);
His truth is marching on. (*Yes sir*)

He has sounded forth the trumpet that shall never call retreat (*Speak sir*);
He is sifting out the hearts of men before His judgment seat. (*That's right*)
O, be swift, my soul, to answer Him! Be jubilant my feet!
Our God is marching on. (*Yeah*)

Glory, hallelujah! (*Yes sir*) Glory, hallelujah! (*All right*)
Glory, hallelujah! Glory, hallelujah!
His truth is marching on. [*Applause*]

DELIVERED IN MONTGOMERY, ALABAMA,
25 MARCH 1965.

BEYOND VIETNAM

**INTRODUCTION BY AMBASSADOR
GEORGE McGOVERN**

erhaps the only issue of the 1960s whose passion rivaled that of the Civil Rights Movement was the ongoing conflict in Vietnam. From the mid-sixties to the mid-seventies, the Vietnam War became the transcendent issue in American politics, and when it combined with the Civil Rights Movement, that decade—from 1965 to 1975—became as divisive as any that had gripped the nation since the Civil War.

Supporters of the United States' participation in the war saw it as a necessary effort to halt the spread of communism in Asia as directed from communist China and the Soviet Union. If Vietnam came to be ruled by the communist leader Ho Chi Minh, they believed, the communist infection would spread to neighboring countries across much of Asia. Acting on the so-called "domino theory," they argued that if the first domino (Vietnam) fell to communism, the country next door would follow suit and then the next and the next, etc.

Those of us who opposed the U.S. involvement in Vietnam took a sharply different view of the issue. Vietnam was a longtime French colony striving to win its independence; Ho Chi Minh, the leader of that movement, was admittedly a communist, but he was first and foremost a popular, courageous champion of Vietnamese independence. We saw the U.S. military intervention as a misguided effort that devastated the Vietnamese countryside, destroyed life in the villages, corrupted Vietnamese politics, and maimed and killed tens of thousands of young Americans and hundreds of thousands of Vietnamese. We also believed that, in the end, the American troop involvement—half a million men—and the aerial bombardment, which exceeded that of the Second World War, would fail. Indeed, this massive military intervention did fail and the United States finally airlifted our ambassador and his staff from the embassy in Saigon on April 30, 1975.

Many Americans, especially the young, became disillusioned by American politics and foreign policy as a consequence of the Vietnamese experience. They saw the war as a contradiction of American ideals of self-determination, justice, and decency. The disproportionate percentage of black youth called to fight in Vietnam was an obvious gross injustice in this war that had not characterized earlier U.S. wars.

The deepening involvement of the United States in the Vietnam War presented a difficult challenge for Martin Luther King. In the early stages of the war, he and his advisors took the position that the civil rights crisis in American society was so compelling, and Dr. King so uniquely endowed to lead the Civil Rights Movement, that he should not permit his energy and leadership to be diverted by the war.

From 1965 on, a growing number of prominent senators were challenging the U.S. military engagement in the Southeast Asian war. Students, faculty members, clergymen, and some business, professional, and labor members were engaging in teach-ins, protest movements, and petitions to Congress to halt the war.

Dr. King believed, as did most of his advisors, that those other Americans could carry the effort against the war, and that he must continue to hold the civil rights banner. Yet as the war dragged on and the American bombardment increasingly devastated the Vietnamese homeland, Dr. King decided that, as a fighter for justice and humanity, he must publicly state his concern relative to Vietnam.

He sent one of his advisors to see me in the summer of 1967. As a United States senator from South Dakota, I had been speaking out against U.S. involvement in Vietnam for several years. I argued that it was a mistake to send young Americans to die in a civil conflict in which we were largely ignorant of the issues involved. It was doubly a mistake to enter such a conflict against the powerful thrust of nationalism. Ho Chi Minh and his supporters held the banner of Vietnamese independence. They had stood with us against the Japanese invaders of World War II. After the war they resisted and finally defeated the French colonialists in 1954. Unfortunately, we sided with the

French and against Vietnamese independence—the same losing hand that cost fifty-eight thousand American lives after the French withdrew from the scene. French leaders warned us against continuing the struggle of Ho Chi Minh, comparing him to the leadership against George Washington in his fight to achieve independence from the British.

I included these thoughts in my discussion with Dr. King's advisor. As one deeply committed to the civil rights leadership of Dr. King, I expressed the view that we also needed his strong moral voice in the effort to end the war.

The emissary said Dr. King was seriously considering a possible statement on the moral issues raised by the war, but that he wanted to avoid the more political aspects of the war issue. Dr. King was aware, however, that the economic cost of the war was jeopardizing domestic programs that were important to his special constituency: the poor, minorities, women, and children. In a sense, every bomb or shell that fell on a Vietnamese target also reduced the education, housing, and health of vulnerable Americans. Dollars used for killing, maiming, and destruction in Vietnam were taken from programs here at home that were meant to improve conditions of life for Americans.

Dr. King enunciated similar views in "Beyond Vietnam," the brilliant speech he eventually delivered in New York City, a speech that reiterated the importance of nonviolent social change and his deep commitment to equal rights for all humanity. Had he not been assassinated in the spring of 1968, I have no doubt his voice would have been joined even more intently against a war that did not finally end until the spring of 1975.

GEORGE MCGOVERN, 1972 Democratic presidential candidate and opponent of the United States' involvement in Vietnam, is the U.S. representative to the United Nations Food and Agricultural Organization.

Beyond
Vietnam

Mr. Chairman, ladies and gentlemen, I need not pause to say how very delighted I am to be here tonight, and how very delighted I am to see you expressing your concern about the issues that will be discussed tonight by turning out in such large numbers. I also want to say that I consider it a great honor to share this program with Dr. Bennett, Dr. Commager, and Rabbi Heschel, some of the distinguished leaders and personalities of our nation. And of course it's always good to come back to Riverside Church. Over the last eight years, I have had the privilege of preaching here almost every year in that period, and it is always a rich and rewarding experience to come to this great church and this great pulpit.

I come to this magnificent house of worship tonight because my conscience leaves me no other choice. I join you in this meeting because I am in deepest agreement with the aims and work of the organization which has brought us together, Clergy and Laymen Concerned About Vietnam. The recent statements of your executive committee are the sentiments of my own heart, and I found myself in full accord when I read its opening lines: "A time comes when silence is betrayal." That time has come for us in relation to Vietnam.

The truth of these words is beyond doubt, but the mission to which they call us is a most difficult one. Even when pressed by the demands of inner truth, men do not easily assume the task of opposing their government's policy, especially in time of war. Nor does the human spirit move without great difficulty against all the apathy of conformist thought within one's own bosom and in the surrounding world. Moreover, when the issues at hand seem as perplexing as they often do in the case of this dreadful conflict, we are always on the verge of being mesmerized by uncertainty. But we must move on.

Some of us who have already begun to break the silence of the night have found that the calling to speak is often a vocation of agony, but we must speak. We must speak with all the humility that is appropriate to our limited vision, but we must speak. And we must rejoice as well, for surely this is the first time in our nation's history that a significant number of its religious leaders have chosen to move beyond the prophesying of smooth patriotism to the high grounds of a firm dissent based upon the mandates of conscience and the reading of history. Perhaps a new spirit is rising among us. If it is, let us trace its movements and pray that our own inner being may be sensitive to its guidance. For we are deeply in need of a new way beyond the darkness that seems so close around us.

Over the past two years, as I have moved to break the betrayal of my own silences and to speak from the burnings of my own heart, as I have called for radical departures from the destruction of Vietnam, many persons have questioned me about the wisdom of my path. At the heart of their concerns, this query has often loomed large and loud: "Why are you speaking about the war, Dr. King? Why are you joining the voices of dissent?" "Peace and civil rights don't mix," they say. "Aren't you hurting the cause of your people?" they ask. And when I hear them, though I often understand the source of their concern, I am nevertheless greatly saddened, for such questions mean that the inquirers have not really known me, my commitment, or my calling. Indeed, their questions suggest that they do not know the world in which they live. In the light of such tragic misunderstanding, I deem it of signal importance to try to state clearly, and I trust concisely, why I believe that the path from Dexter Avenue Baptist Church—the church in Montgomery, Alabama, where I began my pastorate—leads clearly to this sanctuary tonight.

I come to this platform tonight to make a passionate plea to my beloved nation. This speech is not addressed to Hanoi or to the National Liberation Front. It is not addressed to China or to Russia. Nor is it an attempt to overlook the ambiguity of the total situation and the need for a collective solution to the tragedy of Vietnam. Neither is it an attempt to make North Vietnam or the National Liberation Front paragons of virtue, nor to overlook the role they must play in the successful resolution of the problem. While they both may have justifiable reasons to be suspicious of the good faith of the United States, life and history give eloquent testimony to the fact that conflicts are never resolved without trustful give and take on both sides. Tonight, however, I wish not to speak with Hanoi and the National Liberation Front, but rather to my fellow Americans.

Since I am a preacher by calling, I suppose it is not surprising that I have seven major reasons for bringing Vietnam into the field of my moral vision. There is at the outset a very obvious and almost facile connection between the war in Vietnam and the struggle I and others have been waging in America. A few years ago there was a shining moment in that struggle. It seemed as if there was a real promise of hope for the poor, both black and white, through the poverty program. There were experiments, hopes, new beginnings. Then came the buildup in Vietnam, and I watched this program broken and eviscerated as if it were some idle political plaything of a society gone mad on war. And I knew that America would never invest the necessary funds or energies in rehabilitation of its poor so long as adventures like Vietnam continued to draw men and skills and money like some demonic, destructive suction tube. So I was increasingly compelled to see the war as an enemy of the poor and to attack it as such.

Perhaps a more tragic recognition of reality took place when it became clear to me that the war was doing far more than devastating the hopes of the poor at home. It was sending their sons and their brothers and their husbands to fight and to die in extraordinarily high proportions relative to the rest of the population. We were taking the black young men who had been crippled by our society and sending them eight thousand miles away to guarantee liberties in Southeast Asia which they had not found in southwest Georgia and East Harlem. So we have been repeatedly faced with the cruel irony of watching Negro and white boys on TV screens as they kill and die together for a nation that has been unable to seat them together in the same schools. So we watch them in brutal solidarity burning the huts of a poor village, but we realize that they would hardly live on the same block in Chicago. I could not be silent in the face of such cruel manipulation of the poor.

My third reason moves to an even deeper level of awareness, for it grows out of my experience in the ghettos of the North over the last three years, especially the last three summers. As I have walked among the desperate, rejected, and angry young men, I have told them that Molotov cocktails and rifles would not solve their problems. I have tried to offer them my deepest compassion while maintaining my conviction that social change comes most meaningfully through nonviolent action. But they asked, and rightly so, "What about Vietnam?" They asked if our own nation wasn't using massive doses of violence to solve its problems, to bring about the changes it wanted. Their questions hit home, and I knew that I could never again raise my voice against the violence of the oppressed in the ghettos without having first spoken clearly to the greatest purveyor of violence in the world today: my own government. For the sake of those boys, for the sake of this government, for the sake of the hundreds of thousands trembling under our violence, I cannot be silent.

For those who ask the question, "Aren't you a civil rights leader?" and thereby mean to exclude me from the movement for peace, I have this further answer. In 1957, when a group of us formed the Southern Christian Leadership Conference, we chose as our motto: "To save the soul of America." We were convinced that we could not limit our vision to certain rights for black people, but instead affirmed the conviction that America would never be free or saved from itself until the descendants of its slaves were loosed completely from the shackles they still wear. In a way we were agreeing with Langston Hughes, that black bard of Harlem, who had written earlier:

> O, yes, I say it plain,
> America never was America to me,
> And yet I swear this oath—
> America will be!

Now it should be incandescently clear that no one who has any concern for the integrity and life of America today can ignore the present war. If America's soul becomes totally poisoned, part of the autopsy must read "Vietnam." It can never be saved so long as it destroys the deepest hopes of men the world over. So it is that those of us who are yet determined that "America will be" are led down the path of protest and dissent, working for the health of our land.

As if the weight of such a commitment to the life

and health of America were not enough, another burden of responsibility was placed upon me in [1964]. And I cannot forget that the Nobel Peace Prize was also a commission, a commission to work harder than I had ever worked before for the brotherhood of man. This is a calling that takes me beyond national allegiances.

But even if it were not present, I would yet have to live with the meaning of my commitment to the ministry of Jesus Christ. To me, the relationship of this ministry to the making of peace is so obvious that I sometimes marvel at those who ask me why I am speaking against the war. Could it be that they do not know that the Good News was meant for all men—for communist and capitalist, for their children and ours, for black and for white, for revolutionary and conservative? Have they forgotten that my ministry is in obedience to the one who loved his enemies so fully that he died for them? What then can I say to the Vietcong or to Castro or to Mao as a faithful minister of this one? Can I threaten them with death or must I not share with them my life?

Finally, as I try to explain for you and for myself the road that leads from Montgomery to this place, I would have offered all that was most valid if I simply said that I must be true to my conviction that I share with all men the calling to be a son of the living God. Beyond the calling of race or nation or creed is this vocation of sonship and brotherhood. Because I believe that the Father is deeply concerned, especially for His suffering and helpless and outcast children, I come tonight to speak for them. This I believe to be the privilege and the burden of all of us who deem ourselves bound by allegiances and loyalties which are broader and deeper than nationalism and which go beyond our nation's self-defined goals and positions. We are called to speak for the weak, for the voiceless, for the victims of our nation, for those it calls "enemy," for no document from human hands can make these humans any less our brothers.

And as I ponder the madness of Vietnam and search within myself for ways to understand and respond in compassion, my mind goes constantly to the people of that peninsula. I speak now not of the soldiers of each side, not of the ideologies of the Liberation Front, not of the junta in Saigon, but simply of the people who have been living under the curse of war for almost three continuous decades now. I think of them, too, because it is clear to me that there will be no meaningful solution there until some attempt is made to know them and hear their broken cries.

They must see Americans as strange liberators. The Vietnamese people proclaimed their own independence in 1954—in 1945 rather—after a combined French and Japanese occupation and before the communist revolution in China. They were led by Ho Chi Minh. Even though they quoted the American Declaration of Independence in their own document of freedom, we refused to recognize them. Instead, we decided to support France in its reconquest of her former colony. Our government felt then that the Vietnamese people were not ready for independence, and we again fell victim to the deadly Western arrogance that has poisoned the international atmosphere for so long. With that tragic decision we rejected a revolutionary government seeking self-determination and a government that had been established not by China—for whom the Vietnamese have no great love—but by clearly indigenous forces that included some communists. For the peasants this new government meant real land reform, one of the most important needs in their lives.

For nine years following 1945 we denied the people of Vietnam the right of independence. For nine years we vigorously supported the French in their abortive effort to recolonize Vietnam. Before the end of the war we were meeting 80 percent of the French war costs. Even before the French were defeated at Dien Bien Phu, they began to despair of their reckless action, but we did not. We encouraged them with our huge financial and military supplies to continue the war even after they had lost the will. Soon we would be paying almost the full costs of this tragic attempt at recolonization.

After the French were defeated, it looked as if independence and land reform would come again through the Geneva Agreement. But instead there came the United States, determined that Ho should not unify the temporarily divided nation, and the peasants watched again as we supported one of the most vicious modern dictators, our chosen man, Premier Diem. The peasants watched and cringed as Diem ruthlessly rooted out all opposition, supported their extortionist landlords, and refused even to discuss reunification with the North. The peasants watched as all of this was presided over by United

States influence and then by increasing numbers of United States troops who came to help quell the insurgency that Diem's methods had aroused. When Diem was overthrown they may have been happy, but the long line of military dictators seemed to offer no real change, especially in terms of their need for land and peace.

The only change came from America as we increased our troop commitments in support of governments which were singularly corrupt, inept, and without popular support. All the while the people read our leaflets and received the regular promises of peace and democracy and land reform. Now they languish under our bombs and consider us, not their fellow Vietnamese, the real enemy. They move sadly and apathetically as we herd them off the land of their fathers into concentration camps where minimal social needs are rarely met. They know they must move on or be destroyed by our bombs.

So they go, primarily women and children and the aged. They watch as we poison their water, as we kill a million acres of their crops. They must weep as the bulldozers roar through their areas preparing to destroy the precious trees. They wander into the hospitals with at least twenty casualties from American firepower for one Vietcong-inflicted injury. So far we may have killed a million of them, mostly children. They wander into the towns and see thousands of the children, homeless, without clothes, running in packs on the streets like animals. They see the children degraded by our soldiers as they beg for food. They see the children selling their sisters to our soldiers, soliciting for their mothers.

What do the peasants think as we ally ourselves with the landlords and as we refuse to put any action into our many words concerning land reform? What do they think as we test out our latest weapons on them, just as the Germans tested out new medicine and new tortures in the concentration camps of Europe? Where are the roots of the independent Vietnam we claim to be building? Is it among these voiceless ones?

We have destroyed their two most cherished institutions: the family and the village. We have destroyed their land and their crops. We have cooperated in the crushing of the nation's only noncommunist revolutionary political force, the unified Buddhist Church. We have supported the enemies of the peasants of Saigon. We have corrupted their women and children and killed their men.

Now there is little left to build on, save bitterness. Soon the only solid physical foundations remaining will be found at our military bases and in the concrete of the concentration camps we call "fortified hamlets." The peasants may well wonder if we plan to build our new Vietnam on such grounds as these. Could we blame them for such thoughts? We must speak for them and raise the questions they cannot raise. These, too, are our brothers.

Perhaps a more difficult but no less necessary task is to speak for those who have been designated as our enemies. What of the National Liberation Front, that strangely anonymous group we call "VC" or "communists"? What must they think of the United States of America when they realize that we permitted the repression and cruelty of Diem, which helped to bring them into being as a resistance group in the South? What do they think of our condoning the violence which led to their own taking up of arms? How can they believe in our integrity when now we speak of "aggression from the North" as if there were nothing more essential to the war? How can they trust us when now we charge them with violence after the murderous reign of Diem and charge them with violence while we pour every new weapon of death into their land? Surely we must understand their feelings, even if we do not condone their actions. Surely we must see that the men we supported pressed them to their violence. Surely we must see that our own computerized plans of destruction simply dwarf their greatest acts.

How do they judge us when our officials know that their membership is less than 25 percent communist, and yet insist on giving them the blanket name? What must they be thinking when they know that we are aware of their control of major sections of Vietnam, and yet we appear ready to allow national elections in which this highly organized political parallel government will not have a part? They ask how we can speak of free elections when the Saigon press is censored and controlled by the military junta. And they are surely right to wonder what kind of new government we plan to help form without them, the only party in real touch with the peasants. They question our political goals and they deny the reality of a peace settlement from which they will be excluded. Their questions are frighteningly relevant. Is our nation planning to build on political myth again, and then shore it up upon the power of a new violence?

Here is the true meaning and value of compassion and nonviolence, when it helps us to see the enemy's point of view, to hear his questions, to know his assessment of ourselves. For from his view we may indeed see the basic weaknesses of our own condition, and if we are mature, we may learn and grow and profit from the wisdom of the brothers who are called the opposition.

So, too, with Hanoi. In the North, where our bombs now pummel the land, and our mines endanger the waterways, we are met by a deep but understandable mistrust. To speak for them is to explain this lack of confidence in Western words, and especially their distrust of American intentions now. In Hanoi are the men who led the nation to independence against the Japanese and the French, the men who sought membership in the French Commonwealth and were betrayed by the weakness of Paris and the willfulness of the colonial armies. It was they who led a second struggle against French domination at tremendous costs, and then were persuaded to give up the land they controlled between the thirteenth and seventeenth parallel as a temporary measure at Geneva. After 1954 they watched us conspire with Diem to prevent elections which could have surely brought Ho Chi Minh to power over a united Vietnam, and they realized they had been betrayed again.

When we ask why they do not leap to negotiate, these things must be remembered.

Also, it must be clear that the leaders of Hanoi considered the presence of American troops in support of the Diem regime to have been the initial military breach of the Geneva Agreement concerning foreign troops. They remind us that they did not begin to send troops in large numbers and even supplies into the South until American forces had moved into the tens of thousands.

Hanoi remembers how our leaders refused to tell us the truth about the earlier North Vietnamese overtures for peace, how the president claimed that none existed when they had clearly been made. Ho Chi Minh has watched as America has spoken of peace and built up its forces, and now he has surely heard the increasing international rumors of American plans for an invasion of the North. He knows the bombing and shelling and mining we are doing are part of traditional pre-invasion strategy. Perhaps only his sense of humor and of irony can save him when he hears the most powerful nation of the world speaking of aggression as it drops thousands of bombs on a poor, weak nation more than eight hundred, or rather, eight thousand miles away from its shores.

At this point I should make it clear that while I have tried in these last few minutes to give a voice to the voiceless in Vietnam and to understand the arguments of those who are called "enemy," I am as deeply concerned about our own troops there as anything else. For it occurs to me that what we are submitting them to in Vietnam is not simply the brutalizing process that goes on in any war where armies face each other and seek to destroy. We are adding cynicism to the process of death, for they must know after a short period there that none of the things we claim to be fighting for are really involved. Before long they must know that their government has sent them into a struggle among Vietnamese, and the more sophisticated surely realize that we are on the side of the wealthy, and the secure, while we create a hell for the poor.

Somehow this madness must cease. We must stop now. I speak as a child of God and brother to the suffering poor of Vietnam. I speak for those whose land is being laid waste, whose homes are being destroyed, whose culture is being subverted. I speak for the poor of America who are paying the double price of smashed hopes at home, and dealt death and corruption in Vietnam. I speak as a citizen of the world, for the world as it stands aghast at the path we have taken. I speak as one who loves America, to the leaders of our own nation: The great initiative in this war is ours; the initiative to stop it must be ours.

This is the message of the great Buddhist leaders of Vietnam. Recently one of them wrote these words, and I quote:

> Each day the war goes on the hatred increases in the heart of the Vietnamese and in the hearts of those of humanitarian instinct. The Americans are forcing even their friends into becoming their enemies. It is curious that the Americans, who calculate

so carefully on the possibilities of military victory, do not realize that in the process they are incurring deep psychological and political defeat. The image of America will never again be the image of revolution, freedom, and democracy, but the image of violence and militarism.

Unquote.

If we continue, there will be no doubt in my mind and in the mind of the world that we have no honorable intentions in Vietnam. If we do not stop our war against the people of Vietnam immediately, the world will be left with no other alternative than to see this as some horrible, clumsy, and deadly game we have decided to play. The world now demands a maturity of America that we may not be able to achieve. It demands that we admit that we have been wrong from the beginning of our adventure in Vietnam, that we have been detrimental to the life of the Vietnamese people. The situation is one in which we must be ready to turn sharply from our present ways. In order to atone for our sins and errors in Vietnam, we should take the initiative in bringing a halt to this tragic war.

I would like to suggest five concrete things that our government should do immediately to begin the long and difficult process of extricating ourselves from this nightmarish conflict:

Number one: End all bombing in North and South Vietnam.

Number two: Declare a unilateral cease-fire in the

hope that such action will create the atmosphere for negotiation.

Three: Take immediate steps to prevent other battlegrounds in Southeast Asia by curtailing our military buildup in Thailand and our interference in Laos.

Four: Realistically accept the fact that the National Liberation Front has substantial support in South Vietnam and must thereby play a role in any meaningful negotiations and any future Vietnam government.

Five: Set a date that we will remove all foreign troops from Vietnam in accordance with the 1954 Geneva Agreement. [*Sustained applause*]

Part of our ongoing [*Applause continues*], part of our ongoing commitment might well express itself in an offer to grant asylum to any Vietnamese who fears for his life under a new regime which included the Liberation Front. Then we must make what reparations we can for the damage we have done. We must provide the medical aid that is badly needed, making it available in this country if necessary. Meanwhile [*Applause*], meanwhile, we in the churches and synagogues have a continuing task while we urge our government to disengage itself from a disgraceful commitment. We must continue to raise our voices and our lives if our nation persists in its perverse ways in Vietnam. We must be prepared to match actions with words by seeking out every creative method of protest possible.

As we counsel young men concerning military service, we must clarify for them our nation's role in Vietnam and challenge them with the alternative of conscientious objection. [*Sustained applause*] I am pleased to say that this is a path now chosen by more than seventy students at my own alma mater, More-house College, and I recommend it to all who find the American course in Vietnam a dishonorable and unjust one. [*Applause*] Moreover, I would encourage all ministers of draft age to give up their ministerial exemptions and seek status as conscientious objectors. [*Applause*] These are the times for real choices and not false ones. We are at the moment when our lives must be placed on the line if our nation is to survive its own folly. Every man of humane convictions must decide on the protest that best suits his convictions, but we must all protest.

Now there is something seductively tempting about stopping there and sending us all off on what in some circles has become a popular crusade against the war in Vietnam. I say we must enter that struggle, but I wish to go on now to say something even more disturbing.

The war in Vietnam is but a symptom of a far deeper malady within the American spirit, and if we ignore this sobering reality [*Applause*], and if we ignore this sobering reality, we will find ourselves organizing "clergy and laymen concerned" committees for the next generation. They will be concerned about Guatemala and Peru. They will be concerned about Thailand and Cambodia. They will be concerned about Mozambique and South Africa. We will be marching for these and a dozen other names and attending rallies without end unless there is a significant and profound change in American life and policy. [*Sustained applause*] So such thoughts take us beyond

Vietnam, but not beyond our calling as sons of the living God.

In 1957 a sensitive American official overseas said that it seemed to him that our nation was on the wrong side of a world revolution. During the past ten years we have seen emerge a pattern of suppression which has now justified the presence of U.S. military advisors in Venezuela. This need to maintain social stability for our investments accounts for the counterrevolutionary action of American forces in Guatemala. It tells why American helicopters are being used against guerrillas in Cambodia and why American napalm and Green Beret forces have already been active against rebels in Peru.

It is with such activity in mind that the words of the late John F. Kennedy come back to haunt us. Five years ago he said, "Those who make peaceful revolution impossible will make violent revolution inevitable." [*Applause*] Increasingly, by choice or by accident, this is the role our nation has taken, the role of those who make peaceful revolution impossible by refusing to give up the privileges and the pleasures that come from the immense profits of overseas investments. I am convinced that if we are to get on the right side of the world revolution, we as a nation must undergo a radical revolution of values. We must rapidly begin [*Applause*], we must rapidly begin the shift from a thing-oriented society to a person-oriented society. When machines and computers, profit motives and property rights, are considered more important than people, the giant triplets of racism, extreme materialism, and militarism are incapable of being conquered.

A true revolution of values will soon cause us to question the fairness and justice of many of our past and present policies. On the one hand we are called to play the Good Samaritan on life's roadside, but that will be only an initial act. One day we must come to see that the whole Jericho Road must be transformed so that men and women will not be constantly beaten and robbed as they make their journey on life's highway. True compassion is more than flinging a coin to a beggar. It comes to see that an edifice which produces beggars needs restructuring. [*Applause*]

A true revolution of values will soon look uneasily on the glaring contrast of poverty and wealth. With righteous indignation, it will look across the seas and see individual capitalists of the West investing huge sums of money in Asia, Africa, and South America, only to take the profits out with no concern for the social betterment of the countries, and say, "This is not just." It will look at our alliance with the landed gentry of South America and say, "This is not just." The Western arrogance of feeling that it has everything to teach others and nothing to learn from them is not just.

A true revolution of values will lay hand on the world order and say of war, "This way of settling differences is not just." This business of burning human beings with napalm, of filling our nation's homes with orphans and widows, of injecting poisonous drugs of hate into the veins of peoples normally humane, of sending men home from dark and bloody battlefields physically handicapped and psychologically deranged, cannot be reconciled with wisdom, justice, and love. A nation that continues year after year to spend more money on military defense than on programs of social uplift is approaching spiritual death. [*Sustained applause*]

America, the richest and most powerful nation in the world, can well lead the way in this revolution of values. There is nothing except a tragic death wish to prevent us from reordering our priorities so that the pursuit of peace will take precedence over the pursuit of war. There is nothing to keep us from molding a recalcitrant status quo with bruised hands until we have fashioned it into a brotherhood.

This kind of positive revolution of values is our best defense against communism. [*Applause*] War is not the answer. Communism will never be defeated by the use of atomic bombs or nuclear weapons. Let us not join those who shout war and, through their misguided passions, urge the United States to relinquish its participation in the United Nations. These are days which demand wise restraint and calm reasonableness. We must not engage in a negative anticommunism, but rather in a positive thrust for democracy [*Applause*], realizing that our greatest defense against communism is to take offensive action in behalf of justice. We must with positive action seek to remove those conditions of poverty, insecurity, and injustice, which are the fertile soil in which the seed of communism grows and develops.

These are revolutionary times. All over the globe

men are revolting against old systems of exploitation and oppression, and out of the wounds of a frail world, new systems of justice and equality are being born. The shirtless and barefoot people of the land are rising up as never before. The people who sat in darkness have seen a great light. We in the West must support these revolutions.

It is a sad fact that because of comfort, complacency, a morbid fear of communism, and our proneness to adjust to injustice, the Western nations that initiated so much of the revolutionary spirit of the modern world have now become the arch antirevolutionaries. This has driven many to feel that only Marxism has a revolutionary spirit. Therefore, communism is a judgment against our failure to make democracy real and follow through on the revolutions that we initiated. Our only hope today lies in our ability to recapture the revolutionary spirit and go out into a sometimes hostile world declaring eternal hostility to poverty, racism, and militarism. With this powerful commitment we shall boldly challenge the status quo and unjust mores, and thereby speed the day when every valley shall be exalted, and every mountain and hill shall be made low [*Audience:*] (*Yes*); the crooked shall be made straight, and the rough places plain.

A genuine revolution of values means in the final analysis that our loyalties must become ecumenical rather than sectional. Every nation must now develop an overriding loyalty to mankind as a whole in order to preserve the best in their individual societies.

This call for a worldwide fellowship that lifts neighborly concern beyond one's tribe, race, class, and nation is in reality a call for an all-embracing and unconditional love for all mankind. This oft misunderstood, this oft misinterpreted concept, so readily dismissed by the Nietzsches of the world as a weak and cowardly force, has now become an absolute necessity for the survival of man. When I speak of love I am not speaking of some sentimental and weak response. I'm not speaking of that force which is just emotional bosh. I am speaking of that force which all of the great religions have seen as the supreme unifying principle of life. Love is somehow the key that unlocks the door which leads to ultimate reality. This Hindu-Muslim-Christian-Jewish-Buddhist belief about ultimate reality is beautifully summed up in the first epistle of Saint John: "Let us love one another (*Yes*), for love is God. (*Yes*) And every one that loveth is born of God and knoweth God. He that loveth not knoweth not God, for God is love. . . . If we love one another, God dwelleth in us and his love is perfected in us." Let us hope that this spirit will become the order of the day.

We can no longer afford to worship the god of hate or bow before the altar of retaliation. The oceans of history are made turbulent by the ever-rising tides of hate. History is cluttered with the wreckage of nations and individuals that pursued this self-defeating path of hate. As Arnold Toynbee says: "Love is the ultimate force that makes for the saving choice of life and good against the damning choice of death and evil. Therefore the first hope in our inventory must

be the hope that love is going to have the last word."
Unquote.

We are now faced with the fact, my friends, that
tomorrow is today. We are confronted with the fierce
urgency of now. In this unfolding conundrum of life
and history, there is such a thing as being too late.
Procrastination is still the thief of time. Life often
leaves us standing bare, naked, and dejected with a
lost opportunity. The tide in the affairs of men does
not remain at flood—it ebbs. We may cry out des-
perately for time to pause in her passage, but time is
adamant to every plea and rushes on. Over the
bleached bones and jumbled residues of numerous civ-
ilizations are written the pathetic words, "Too late."
There is an invisible book of life that faithfully records
our vigilance or our neglect. Omar Khayyam is right:
"The moving finger writes, and having writ moves
on."

We still have a choice today: nonviolent coexistence
or violent coannihilation. We must move past inde-
cision to action. We must find new ways to speak for
peace in Vietnam and justice throughout the developing world, a world that borders on our doors. If
we do not act, we shall surely be dragged down the
long, dark, and shameful corridors of time reserved
for those who possess power without compassion,
might without morality, and strength without sight.

Now let us begin. Now let us rededicate ourselves
to the long and bitter, but beautiful, struggle for a
new world. This is the calling of the sons of God,
and our brothers wait eagerly for our response. Shall
we say the odds are too great? Shall we tell them the

struggle is too hard? Will our message be that the forces of American life militate against their arrival as full men, and we send our deepest regrets? Or will there be another message—of longing, of hope, of solidarity with their yearnings, of commitment to their cause, whatever the cost? The choice is ours, and though we might prefer it otherwise, we must choose in this crucial moment of human history.

As that noble bard of yesterday James Russell Lowell eloquently stated:

Once to every man and nation comes a moment to
decide,
In the strife of Truth and Falsehood, for the good
or evil side;
Some great cause, God's new Messiah offering each
the bloom or blight,
And the choice goes by forever 'twixt that darkness
and that light.

Though the cause of evil prosper, yet 'tis truth
alone is strong
Though her portions be the scaffold, and upon the
throne be wrong
Yet that scaffold sways the future, and behind the
dim unknown
Standeth God within the shadow, keeping watch
above his own.

And if we will only make the right choice, we will be able to transform this pending cosmic elegy into a creative psalm of peace. If we will make the right choice, we will be able to transform the jangling discords of our world into a beautiful symphony of brotherhood. If we will but make the right choice, we will be able to speed up the day, all over America and all over the world, when justice will roll down like waters, and righteousness like a mighty stream. [*Sustained applause*]

DELIVERED AT RIVERSIDE CHURCH,
NEW YORK, NEW YORK,
4 APRIL 1967.

WHERE DO WE GO FROM HERE?

INTRODUCTION BY SENATOR EDWARD M. KENNEDY

Where Do We Go from Here?" is a timeless and powerful reminder of Martin Luther King, Jr.'s comprehensive vision of racial justice. Too often, when people look back on the history of the Civil Rights Movement, they draw a false distinction between the issues of moral justice and economic justice. As Dr. King understood, we can never fully achieve one without the other. Even now, with the incredible moral force and the inspiration Dr. King provided, when we honor his memory, we too often forget that he was also a champion of economic justice for all Americans.

Unfortunately, much of Dr. King's broad and powerful message is in danger of being left behind as new generations come to know him only through history and see him more as myth than as man. His life and great works are still relevant to the complex realities of today's social problems, and if we allow the richness of his example to recede, we lose the opportunity to continue to learn from him.

There is still much to learn by walking in his path. Change a few words in the speech—replace "Negro" with "African-American"—and readers will think they're reading the work of one of the best and brightest of today's social commentators. His great speech touches on many specific issues that are especially important today, such as economic opportunity, community reinvestment, affordable housing and home ownership, and education. The speech chronicles successful grassroots efforts that are still relevant models for today.

Most important, Dr. King reminds us that the effects of hundreds of years of slavery and segregation cannot be wiped away in just a few years. The thirty-four years since he spoke these words are too short a time to right the wrongs of over two hundred years, particularly when so much of the early wealth of our nation was built on the backs of an enslaved and subjugated minority.

Clearly, we've made great progress since 1967, and all Americans owe Dr. King a tremendous debt of gratitude. But we're still fighting for economic justice and true equality, and it's unfortunate that we often also find ourselves fighting a rearguard action to protect the gains of the past. Despite the fact that minority-owned businesses are still grossly under-used in government contracting, year after year there are fresh assaults on the affirmative action programs that are designed to expand opportunities for minority businesses. Describing Operation Breadbasket, Dr. King said, "'If you respect my dollar, you must respect my person.' It simply says that we will no longer spend our money where we can not get substantial jobs." The same principle applies to tax dollars. Minorities contribute their fair share of taxes to federal and state governments, and minority businesses deserve a full and fair opportunity to compete for government contracts.

Dr. King would have been proud of our contemporary Community Reinvestment Act. The law tells banks that when they accept deposits from low-income and minority neighborhoods, they must invest resources in the same communities. Dr. King was talking about just this type of community investment when he said to Sealtest executives, in essence, you get profits from the African-American community in Cleveland, so you should deposit money in African-American banks in Cleveland and advertise in African-American papers. He was insisting that commerce must be a two-way street, and not just a way to take capital out of minority communities. The Community Reinvestment Act tells banks to do the same thing, and just like Dr. King's efforts with Sealtest, it has been a significant success for banks and communities alike. Banks have developed successful new lines of business by making education and business loans to minorities, and the capital flowing into low-income communities promotes economic expansion. Yet, despite its successes, as we try to modernize our banking and finance laws, some in Congress persist in trying to repeal or weaken the Community Reinvestment Act.

In "Where Do We Go from Here?" Dr. King acknowledged the gains that had been achieved by 1967, but he concentrated on how much was left to do. To draw a stark contrast, he referred to the insulting fact that the Constitution originally counted an enslaved Negro as only 60 percent of a person. In 1967, Dr. King said, African-Americans seemed to count as only 50 percent of a person—they had only half the income of whites, and half lived in substandard housing. They had twice the unemployment rate, and an infant mortality rate twice that of whites.

Likewise, we should acknowledge the gains we have made since 1967, but still concentrate on the work left to do. We have closed some of the income gap, but far from all of it. The median income of African-American households is still only 60 percent that of white households. The percentage of African-American families living below the poverty line is still nearly four times higher than it is for whites, and the unemployment rate for African-Americans is now more than twice that of whites. Thankfully, infant mortality rates have plunged across the board, but they are still more than twice as high for African-Americans as for whites.

So, as Dr. King urged in his speech, we must still ask, where do we go from here? His response then helped bring much of the progress we have achieved over the past three decades, and our similar response now can achieve similar progress in the years ahead. We must continue to insist on equal opportunity for all Americans, regardless of race, gender, ethnic background, or sexual orientation. We must end employment discrimination and ensure that jobs are available for all segments of the community. The minimum wage must be high enough to lift working men and women and their families out of poverty. With the same hope, love, and pride of which Dr. King spoke, we must stay committed to the struggle for justice and equality. Dr. King's dream is our dream too. His inspiring words give us new strength to keep on with his fundamental mission of transforming dark yesterdays into bright tomorrows.

EDWARD M. KENNEDY, a lifelong defender of civil and economic rights, has served as a Democratic senator of Massachusetts since 1962.

Where
Do We Go
from Here?

~❖⟹❮❯⟸❖~

D r. Abernathy, our distinguished vice president, fellow delegates to this, the tenth annual session of the Southern Christian Leadership Conference, my brothers and sisters from not only all over the South, but from all over the United States of America: Ten years ago during the piercing chill of a January day and on the heels of the year-long Montgomery bus boycott, a group of approximately one hundred Negro leaders from across the South assembled in this church and agreed on the need for an organization to be formed that could serve as a channel through which local protest organizations in the South could coordinate their protest activities. It was this meeting that gave birth to the Southern Christian Leadership Conference.

And when our organization was formed ten years ago, racial segregation was still a structured part of the architecture of southern society. Negroes with the pangs of hunger and the anguish of thirst were denied access to the average lunch counter. The downtown restaurants were still off-limits for the black man. Negroes, burdened with the fatigue of travel, were still barred from the motels of the highways and the hotels of the cities. Negro boys and girls in dire need of recreational activities were not allowed to inhale the fresh air of the big city parks. Negroes in desperate need of allowing their mental buckets to sink deep into the wells of knowledge were confronted with a firm no when they sought to use the city libraries. Ten years ago, legislative halls of the South were still ringing loud with such words as "interposition" and "nullification." All types of conniving methods were still being used to keep the Negro from becoming a registered voter. A decade ago, not a single Negro entered the legislative chambers of the South except as a porter or a chauffeur. Ten years ago, all too many Negroes were still harried by day and haunted by night by a corroding sense of fear and a nagging sense of nobody-ness. [*Audience:*] (*Yeah*)

But things are different now. In assault after assault, we caused the sagging walls of segregation to come tumbling down. And during this era the entire edifice of segregation was profoundly shaken. This is an accomplishment whose consequences are deeply felt by every southern Negro in his daily life. It is no longer possible to count the number of public establishments that are open to Negroes. Ten years ago, Negroes seemed almost invisible to the larger society, and the facts of their harsh lives were unknown to the majority of the nation. But today, civil rights is a dominating issue in every state, crowding the pages of the press and the daily conversation of white Americans. In this decade of change, the Negro stood up and confronted his oppressor. He faced the bullies and the guns, the dogs and the tear gas. He put himself squarely before the vicious mobs and moved with strength and dignity toward them and decisively defeated them. And the courage with which he confronted enraged mobs dissolved the stereotype of the grinning, submissive Uncle Tom. He came out of his struggle integrated only slightly in the external society, but powerfully integrated within. This was a victory that had to precede all other gains.

In short, over the last ten years the Negro decided to straighten his back up, realizing that a man cannot ride your back unless it is bent. (*Yes, That's right*) We made our government write new laws to alter some of the cruelest injustices that affected us. We made an indifferent and unconcerned nation rise from lethargy and subpoenaed its conscience to appear before the judgment seat of morality on the whole question of civil rights. We gained manhood in the nation that had always called us "boy." It would be hypocritical indeed if I allowed modesty to forbid my saying that SCLC stood at the forefront of all of the watershed movements that brought these monumental changes in the South. For this, we can feel a legitimate pride. But in spite of a decade of significant progress, the problem is far from solved. The deep rumbling of discontent in our cities is indicative of the fact that the plant of freedom has grown only a bud and not yet a flower.

Before discussing the awesome responsibilities that we face in the days ahead, let us take an inventory of our programmatic action and activities over the past year. Last year as we met in Jackson, Mississippi, we were painfully aware of the struggle of our brothers in Grenada, Mississippi. After living for a hundred or more years under the yoke of total segregation, the Negro citizens of this northern Delta hamlet banded together in nonviolent warfare against racial discrimination under the leadership of our affiliate chapter and organization there. The fact of this nondestructive rebellion was as spectacular as its results. In a few short weeks the Grenada County Movement challenged every aspect of the society's exploitive life. Stores which denied employment were boycotted; voter registration increased by thousands. We can never forget the courageous action of the people of Grenada who moved our nation and its federal courts to powerful action in behalf of school integration, giving Grenada one of the most integrated school systems in America. The battle is far from over, but the black people of Grenada have achieved forty of fifty-three demands through their persistent nonviolent efforts.

Slowly but surely, our southern affiliates continued their building and organizing. Seventy-nine counties conducted voter registration drives, while double that number carried on political education and get-out-the-vote efforts. In spite of press opinions, our staff is still overwhelmingly a southern-based staff. One hundred and five persons have worked across the South under the direction of Hosea Williams. What used to be primarily a voter registration staff is actually a multifaceted program dealing with the total life of the community, from farm cooperatives, business development, tutorials, credit unions, et cetera. Especially to be commended are those ninety-nine communities and their staffs which maintain regular mass meetings throughout the year.

Our Citizenship Education Program continues to lay the solid foundation of adult education and community organization upon which all social change must ultimately rest. This year, five hundred local leaders received training at Dorchester and ten community centers through our Citizenship Education Program. And they were trained in literacy, consumer education, planned parenthood, and many other things. And this program, so ably directed by Mrs. Dorothy Cotton, Mrs. Septima Clark, and their staff of eight persons, continues to cover ten southern states. Our auxiliary feature of C.E.P. is the aid which they have given to poor communities, poor counties, in receiving and establishing O.E.O. projects. With the competent professional guidance of our marvelous staff member Miss Mew Soong-Li, Lowndes and Wilcox counties in Alabama have pioneered in developing outstanding poverty programs totally controlled and operated by residents of the area.

Perhaps the area of greatest concentration of my efforts has been in the cities of Chicago and Cleveland. Chicago has been a wonderful proving ground for our work in the North. There have been no earth-shaking victories, but neither has there been failure. Our open housing marches, which finally brought about an agreement which actually calls the power structure of Chicago to capitulate to the Civil Rights Movement, these marches and the agreement have finally begun to pay off. After the season of delay around election periods, the Leadership Conference, organized to meet our demands for an open city, has finally begun to implement the programs agreed to last summer.

But this is not the most important aspect of our work. As a result of our tenant union organizing, we have begun a four-million-dollar rehabilitation project which will renovate deteriorating buildings and allow their tenants the opportunity to own their own homes. This pilot project was the inspiration for the new home ownership bill, which Senator Percy introduced in Congress only recently.

The most dramatic success in Chicago has been Operation Breadbasket. Through Operation Breadbasket we have now achieved for the Negro community of Chicago more than twenty-two hundred new jobs with an income of approximately eighteen million dollars a year, new income to the Negro community. [*Applause*] But not only have we gotten jobs through Operation Breadbasket in Chicago; there was another area through this economic program, and that was the development of financial institutions which were controlled by Negroes and which were sensitive to problems of economic deprivation of the Negro community. The two banks in Chicago that were interested in helping Negro businessmen were largely unable to loan much because of limited assets. Hi-Lo, one of the chain stores in Chicago, agreed to maintain substantial accounts in the two banks, thus increasing their ability to serve the needs of the Negro community. And I can say to you today that as a result of Operation Breadbasket in Chicago, both of these Negro-operated banks have now more than double their assets, and this has been done in less than a year by the work of Operation Breadbasket. [*Applause*]

In addition, the ministers learned that Negro scavengers had been deprived of significant accounts in the ghetto. Whites controlled even the garbage of Negroes. Consequently, the chain stores agreed to contract with Negro scavengers to service at least the stores in Negro areas. Negro insect and rodent exterminators as well as janitorial services were likewise excluded from major contracts with chain stores. The chain stores also agreed to utilize these services. It also became apparent that chain stores advertised only rarely in Negro-owned community newspapers. This area of neglect was also negotiated, giving community newspapers regular, substantial accounts. And finally, the ministers found that Negro contractors, from painters to masons, from electricians to excavators, had also been forced to remain small by the monopolies of white contractors. Breadbasket negotiated agreements on new construction and rehabilitation work for the chain stores. These several interrelated aspects of economic development, all based on the power of organized consumers, hold great possibilities for dealing with the problems of Negroes in other northern cities. The kinds of requests made by Breadbasket in Chicago can be made not only of chain stores, but of almost any major industry in any city in the country.

And so Operation Breadbasket has a very simple program, but a powerful one. It simply says, "If you respect my dollar, you must respect my person." It simply says that we will no longer spend our money where we can not get substantial jobs. [*Applause*]

In Cleveland, Ohio, a group of ministers have formed an Operation Breadbasket through our program there and have moved against a major dairy company. Their requests include jobs, advertising in Negro newspapers, and depositing funds in Negro financial institutions. This effort resulted in something marvelous. I went to Cleveland just last week to sign the agreement with Sealtest. We went to get the facts about their employment. We discovered that they had 442 employees and only forty-three were Negroes, yet the Negro population of Cleveland is 35 percent of the total population. They refused to give us all of the information that we requested, and we said in substance: "Mr. Sealtest, we're sorry. We aren't going to burn your store down. We aren't going to throw any bricks in the window. But we are going to put picket signs around and we are going to put leaflets out and we are going to our pulpits and tell them not to sell Sealtest products, and not to purchase Sealtest products."

We did that. We went through the churches. Reverend Doctor Hoover, who pastors the largest church in Cleveland, who's here today, and all of the ministers got together and got behind this program. We went to every store in the ghetto and said: "You must take Sealtest products off of your counters. If not, we're going to boycott your whole store." A&P refused. We put picket lines around A&P; they have a hundred and some stores in Cleveland, and we picketed A&P and closed down eighteen of them in one day. Nobody went in A&P. [*Applause*] The next day Mr. A&P was calling on us, and Bob Brown, who is here on our board and who is a public relations man representing a number of firms, came in. They called him in because he works for A&P also; and they didn't know he worked for us, too. [*Laughter*] Bob Brown sat down with A&P, and he said, they said, "Now, Mr. Brown, what would you advise us to do?" He said, "I would advise you to take Sealtest products off of all of your counters." A&P agreed next day not only to take Sealtest products off of the counters in the ghetto, but off of the counters of every store, A&P store in Cleveland, and they said to Sealtest, "If you don't reach an agreement with SCLC and Operation Breadbasket, we will take Sealtest products off of every A&P store in the state of Ohio."

The next day [*Applause*], the next day the Sealtest people were talking nice [*Laughter*], they were very humble. And I am proud to say that I went to Cleveland just last Tuesday, and I sat down with the Sealtest people and some seventy ministers from Cleveland, and we signed the agreement. This effort resulted in a number of jobs, which will bring almost $500,000 of new income to the Negro community a year. [*Applause*] We also said to Sealtest: "The problem that we face is that the ghetto is a domestic colony that's constantly drained without being replenished. And you are always telling us to lift ourselves by our own bootstraps, and yet we are being robbed every day. Put something back in the ghetto." So along with our demand for jobs, we said, "We also demand that you put money in the Negro savings and loan association and that you take ads, advertise, in the Cleveland *Call & Post*, the Negro newspaper." So along with the new jobs, Sealtest has now deposited thousands of dollars in the Negro bank of Cleveland and has already started taking ads in the Negro newspaper in that city. This is the power of Operation Breadbasket. [*Applause*]

Now for fear you may feel that it's limited to Chicago and Cleveland, let me say to you that we've gotten even more than that, in Atlanta, Georgia. Breadbasket has been equally successful in the South. Here the emphasis has been divided between governmental employment and private industry. And while I do not have time to go into the details, I want to commend the men who have been working with it here: the Reverend Bennette, the Reverend Joe Boone, the Reverend J. C. Ward, Reverend Dorsey, Reverend Greer, and I could go on down the line. And they have stood up along with all of the other ministers. But here is the story that's not printed in the newspapers in Atlanta: As a result of Operation Breadbasket, over the last three years, we have added about twenty-five million dollars of new income to the Negro community every year. [*Applause*] Now, as you know, Operation Breadbasket has now gone national in the sense that we had a national conference in Chicago and agreed to launch a nationwide program, which you will hear more about.

Finally, SCLC has entered the field of housing. Under the leadership of attorney James Robinson, we have already contracted to build 152 units of low-income housing with apartments for the elderly on a choice downtown Atlanta site under the sponsorship of Ebenezer Baptist Church. This is the first project [*Applause*], this is the first project of a proposed south-wide Housing Development Corporation which we hope to develop in conjunction with SCLC, and through this corporation we hope to build housing from Mississippi to North Carolina using Negro workmen, Negro architects, Negro attorneys, and Negro financial institutions throughout. And it is our feeling that in the next two or three years, we can build right here in the South forty million dollars' worth of new housing for Negroes, and with millions and millions of dollars in income coming to the Negro community. [*Applause*] Now there are many other things that I could tell you, but time is passing. This, in short, is an account of SCLC's work over the last year. It is a record of which we can all be proud.

With all the struggle and all the achievements, we must face the fact, however, that the Negro still lives in the basement of the Great Society. He is still at the bottom, despite the few who have penetrated to slightly higher levels. Even where the door has been forced partially open, mobility for the Negro is still sharply restricted. There is often no bottom at which to start, and when there is there's almost no room at the top. In consequence, Negroes are still impoverished aliens in an affluent society. They are too poor even to rise with the society, too impoverished by the ages to be able to ascend by using their own resources. And the Negro did not do this himself; it was done to him. For more than half of his American history, he was enslaved. Yet he built the spanning bridges, the grand mansions, the sturdy docks, and stout factories of the South. His unpaid labor made cotton king and established America as a significant nation in international commerce. Even after his release from chattel slavery, the nation grew over him, submerging him. It became the richest, most powerful society in the history of man, but it left the Negro far behind.

And so we still have a long, long way to go before we reach the promised land of freedom. Yes, we have left the dusty soils of Egypt, and we have crossed a Red Sea that had for years been hardened by a long and piercing winter of massive resistance, but before we reach the majestic shores of the Promised Land, there will still be gigantic mountains of opposition ahead and prodigious hilltops of injustice. (*That's right*) We still need some Paul Revere of conscience to alert every hamlet and every village of America that revolution is still at hand. Yes, we need a chart; we need a compass; indeed, we need some North Star to guide us into a future shrouded with impenetrable uncertainties.

Now in order to answer the question, "Where do we go from here?" which is our theme, we must first honestly recognize where we are now. When the Constitution was written, a strange formula to determine taxes and representation declared that the Negro was 60 percent of a person. Today another curious formula seems to declare he is 50 percent of a person. Of the good things in life, the Negro has approximately one half those of whites. Of the bad things of life, he has twice those of whites. Thus, half of all Negroes live in substandard housing. And Negroes have half the income of whites. When we turn to the negative experiences of life, the Negro has a double share: There are twice as many unemployed; the rate of infant mortality among Negroes is double that of whites; and there are twice as many Negroes dying in Vietnam as whites in proportion to their size in the population. [*Applause*]

In other spheres, the figures are equally alarming. In elementary schools, Negroes lag one to three years behind whites, and their segregated schools (*Yeah*) receive substantially less money per student than the white schools. (*Those schools*) One-twentieth as many Negroes as whites attend college. Of employed Negroes, 75 percent hold menial jobs. This is where we are.

Where do we go from here? First, we must massively assert our dignity and worth. We must stand up amid a system that still oppresses us and develop an unassailable and majestic sense of values. We must no longer be ashamed of being black. The job of arousing manhood within a people that have been taught for so many centuries that they are nobody is not easy.

Even semantics have conspired to make that which is black seem ugly and degrading. (*Yes*) In Roget's *Thesaurus* there are some 120 synonyms for blackness and at least sixty of them are offensive, such words as blot, soot, grim, devil, and foul. And there are some 134 synonyms for whiteness and all are favorable, expressed in such words as purity, cleanliness, chastity, and innocence. A white lie is better than a black lie. (*Yes*) The most degenerate member of a family is the "black sheep." (*Yes*) Ossie Davis has suggested that maybe the English language should be reconstructed so that teachers will not be forced to teach the Negro child sixty ways to despise himself and thereby perpetuate his false sense of inferiority, and the white child 134 ways to adore himself and thereby perpetuate his false sense of superiority. [*Applause*] The tendency to ignore the Negro's contribution to American life and strip him of his personhood is as old as the earliest history books and as contemporary as the morning's newspaper.

To offset this cultural homicide, the Negro must rise up with an affirmation of his own Olympian manhood. (*Yes*) Any movement for the Negro's freedom that overlooks this necessity is only waiting to be buried. (*Yes*) As long as the mind is enslaved, the body can never be free. (*Yes*) Psychological freedom, a firm sense of self-esteem, is the most powerful weapon against the long night of physical slavery. No Lincolnian Emancipation Proclamation, no Johnsonian civil rights bill can totally bring this kind of freedom. The Negro will only be free when he reaches down to the inner depths of his own being and signs with the pen and ink of assertive manhood his own emancipation proclamation. And with a spirit straining toward true self-esteem, the Negro must boldly throw off the manacles of self-abnegation and say to himself and to the world, "I am somebody. (*Oh yeah*) I am a person. I am a man with dignity and honor. (*Go ahead*) I have a rich and noble history, however painful and exploited that history has been. Yes, I was a slave through my foreparents, and now I'm not ashamed of that. I'm ashamed of the people who were so sinful to make me a slave." (*Yes sir*) Yes [*Applause*], yes, we must stand up and say, "I'm black, but I'm black and beautiful." (*Yes*) This [*Applause*], this self-affirmation is the black man's need, made compelling (*All right*) by the white man's crimes against him.

Now another basic challenge is to discover how to organize our strength into economic and political power. No one can deny that the Negro is in dire need of this kind of legitimate power. Indeed, one of the great problems that the Negro confronts is his lack of power. From the old plantations of the South to the newer ghettos of the North, the Negro has been confined to a life of voicelessness (*That's true*) and powerlessness. (*So true*) Stripped of the right to make decisions concerning his life and destiny, he has been subject to the authoritarian and sometimes whimsical decisions of the white power structure. The plantation and the ghetto were created by those who had power, both to confine those who had no power and to perpetuate their powerlessness. Now the problem of transforming the ghetto, therefore, is a problem of power, a confrontation between the forces of power demanding change and the forces of power dedicated to the preserving of the status quo. Now, power properly understood is nothing but the ability to achieve purpose. It is the strength required to bring about social, political, and economic change. Walter Reuther defined power one day. He said, "Power is the ability of a labor union like UAW to make the most powerful corporation in the world, General Motors, say 'Yes' when it wants to say 'No.' That's power." [*Applause*]

Now a lot of us are preachers, and all of us have our moral convictions and concerns, and so often we have problems with power. There is nothing wrong with power if power is used correctly. You see, what happened is that some of our philosophers got off base. And one of the great problems of history is that the concepts of love and power have usually been contrasted as opposites, polar opposites, so that love is identified with a resignation of power, and power with a denial of love. It was this misinterpretation that caused the philosopher Nietzsche, who was a philosopher of the will to power, to reject the Christian concept of love. It was this same misinterpretation which induced Christian theologians to reject Nietzsche's philosophy of the will to power in the name of the Christian idea of love.

Now we got to get this thing right. What is needed is a realization that power without love is reckless and abusive, and that love without power is sentimental and anemic. (*Yes*) Power at its best (*Speak*) [*Applause*], power at its best is love (*Yes*) implementing the demands of justice, and justice at its best is love correcting everything that stands against love. (*Speak*) And this is what we must see as we move on.

Now what has happened is that we've had it wrong and mixed up in our country, and this has led Negro Americans in the past to seek their goals through love and moral suasion devoid of power, and white Americans to seek their goals through power devoid of love and conscience. It is leading a few extremists today to advocate for Negroes the same destructive and conscienceless power that they have justly abhorred in whites. It is precisely this collision of immoral power with powerless morality which constitutes the major crisis of our times.

Now we must develop progress, or rather, a program—and I can't stay on this long—that will drive the nation to a guaranteed annual income. Now early in the century this proposal would have been greeted with ridicule and denunciation as destructive of initiative and responsibility. At that time economic status was considered the measure of the individual's abilities and talents. And in the thinking of that day, the absence of worldly goods indicated a want of industrious habits and moral fiber. We've come a long way in our understanding of human motivation and of the blind operation of our economic system. Now we realize that dislocations in the market operation of our economy and the prevalence of discrimination thrust people into idleness and bind them in constant or frequent unemployment against their will. The poor are less often dismissed, I hope, from our conscience today by being branded as inferior and incompetent. We also know that no matter how dynamically the economy develops and expands, it does not eliminate all poverty.

The problem indicates that our emphasis must be twofold: We must create full employment, or we must create incomes. People must be made consumers by one method or the other. Once they are placed in this position, we need to be concerned that the potential of the individual is not wasted. New forms of work that enhance the social good will have to be devised for those for whom traditional jobs are not available. In 1879 Henry George anticipated this state of affairs when he wrote in *Progress and Poverty*:

> The fact is that the work which improves the condition of mankind, the work which extends knowledge and increases power and enriches literature and elevates thought, is not done to secure a living. It is not the work of slaves driven to their tasks either by the task of that of a taskmaster or by animal necessities. It is the work of men who somehow find a form of work that brings a security for its own sake and a state of society where want is abolished.

Work of this sort could be enormously increased, and we are likely to find that the problem of housing, education, instead of preceding the elimination of poverty, will themselves be affected if poverty is first abolished. The poor, transformed into purchasers, will do a great deal on their own to alter housing decay. Negroes, who have a double disability, will have a greater effect on discrimination when they have the additional weapon of cash to use in their struggle.

Beyond these advantages, a host of positive psychological changes inevitably will result from widespread economic security. The dignity of the individual will flourish when the decisions concerning his life are in his own hands, when he has the assurance that his income is stable and certain, and when he knows that he has the means to seek self-improvement. Personal conflicts between husband, wife, and children will diminish when the unjust measurement of human worth on a scale of dollars is eliminated.

Now our country can do this. John Kenneth Galbraith said that a guaranteed annual income could be done for about twenty billion dollars a year. And I say to you today, that if our nation can spend thirty-five billion dollars a year to fight an unjust, evil war in Vietnam, and twenty billion dollars to put a man on the moon, it can spend billions of dollars to put God's children on their own two feet right here on earth. [*Applause*]

Now let me rush on to say we must reaffirm our commitment to nonviolence. And I want to stress this. The futility of violence in the struggle for racial justice has been tragically etched in all the recent Negro riots. Now yesterday, I tried to analyze the riots and deal with the causes for them. Today I want to give the other side. There is something painfully sad about a riot. One sees screaming youngsters and angry adults fighting hopelessly and aimlessly against impossible odds. (*Yeah*) Deep down within them, you perceive a desire for self-destruction, a kind of suicidal longing. (*Yes*)

Occasionally, Negroes contend that the 1965 Watts riot and the other riots in various cities represented effective civil rights action. But those who express this view always end up with stumbling words when asked what concrete gains have been won as a result. At best the riots have produced a little additional anti-poverty money allotted by frightened government officials, and a few water sprinklers to cool the children of the ghettos. It is something like improving the food in the prison while the people remain securely incarcerated behind bars. (*That's right*) Nowhere have the riots won any concrete improvement such as have the organized protest demonstrations.

And when one tries to pin down advocates of violence as to what acts would be effective, the answers are blatantly illogical. Sometimes they talk of overthrowing racist state and local governments and they talk about guerrilla warfare. They fail to see that no internal revolution has ever succeeded in overthrowing a government by violence unless the government had already lost the allegiance and effective control of its armed forces. Anyone in his right mind knows that this will not happen in the United States. In a violent racial situation, the power structure has the local police, the state troopers, the National Guard, and finally, the Army to call on, all of which are predominantly white. (*Yes*) Furthermore, few, if any, violent revolutions have been successful unless the violent minority had the sympathy and support of the nonresisting majority. Castro may have had only a few Cubans actually fighting with him and up in the hills (*Yes*), but he would have never overthrown the Batista regime unless he had had the sympathy of the vast majority of Cuban people. It is perfectly clear that a violent revolution on the part of American blacks would find no sympathy and support from the white population and very little from the majority of the Negroes themselves.

This is no time for romantic illusions and empty philosophical debates about freedom. This is a time for action. (*All right*) What is needed is a strategy for change, a tactical program that will bring the Negro into the mainstream of American life as quickly as possible. So far, this has only been offered by the non-violent movement. Without recognizing this we will end up with solutions that don't solve, answers that don't answer, and explanations that don't explain. [*Applause*]

And so I say to you today that I still stand by non-violence. (*Yes*) And I am still convinced [*Applause*], and I'm still convinced that it is the most potent weapon available to the Negro in his struggle for justice in this country.

And the other thing is, I'm concerned about a better world. I'm concerned about justice; I'm concerned about brotherhood; I'm concerned about truth. And when one is concerned about that, he can never advocate violence. For through violence you may murder a murderer, but you can't murder murder. Through violence you may murder a liar, but you can't establish truth. Through violence you may murder a hater, but you can't murder hate through violence. (*All right, That's right*) Darkness cannot put out darkness; only light can do that. [*Applause*]

And I say to you, I have also decided to stick with love, for I know that love is ultimately the only answer to mankind's problems. And I'm going to talk about it everywhere I go. I know it isn't popular to talk about it in some circles today. And I'm not talking about emotional bosh when I talk about love; I'm talking about a strong, demanding love. For I have seen too much hate. I've seen too much hate on the faces of sheriffs in the South. (*Yeah*) I've seen hate on the faces of too many Klansmen and too many White Citizens' Councilors in the South to want to hate, myself, because every time I see it, I know that it does something to their faces and their personalities, and I say to myself that hate is too great a burden to bear. (*Yes*) I have decided to love. [*Applause*] If you are seeking the highest good, I think you can find it through love. And the beautiful thing is that we aren't moving wrong when we do it, because John was right, God is love. (*Yes*) He who hates does not know God, but he who loves has the key that unlocks the door to the meaning of ultimate reality.

And so I say to you today, my friends, that you may be able to speak with the tongues of men and angels (*All right*), you may have the eloquence of articulate speech; but if you have not love, it means nothing. (*That's right*) Yes, you may have the gift of prophecy, you may have the gift of scientific prediction (*Yes sir*) and understand the behavior of molecules (*All right*), you may break into the storehouse of nature (*Yes sir*) and bring forth many new insights; yes, you may ascend to the heights of academic achievement (*Yes sir*) so that you have all knowledge (*Yes sir, Yes*), and you may boast of your great institutions of learning and the boundless extent of your degrees; but if you have not love, all of these mean absolutely nothing. (*Yes*) You may even give your goods to feed the poor (*Yes sir*), you may bestow great gifts to charity (*Speak*), and you may tower high in philanthropy; but if you have not love, your charity means nothing. (*Yes sir*) You may even give your body to be burned and die the death of a martyr, and your spilt blood may be a symbol of honor for generations yet unborn, and thousands may praise you as one of history's greatest heroes; but if you have not love (*Yes, All right*), your blood was spilt in vain. What I'm trying to get you to see this morning is that a man may be self-centered in his self-denial and self-righteous in his self-sacrifice. His generosity may feed his ego, and his piety may feed his pride. (*Speak*) So without love, benevolence becomes egotism, and martyrdom becomes spiritual pride.

I want to say to you as I move to my conclusion, as we talk about "Where do we go from here?" that we must honestly face the fact that the movement must address itself to the question of restructuring the whole of American society. There are forty million poor people here, and one day we must ask the question, "Why are there forty million poor people in America?" And when you begin to ask that question, you are raising a question about the economic system, about a broader distribution of wealth. When you ask that question, you begin to question the capitalistic economy. (*Yes*) And I'm simply saying that more and more, we've got to begin to ask questions about the whole society. We are called upon to help the discouraged beggars in life's marketplace. (*Yes*) But one day we must come to see that an edifice which produces beggars needs restructuring. (*All right*) It means that questions must be raised. And you see, my friends, when you deal with this you begin to ask the question, "Who owns the oil?" (*Yes*) You begin to ask the question, "Who owns the iron ore?" (*Yes*) You begin to ask the question, "Why is it that people have to pay water bills in a world that's two-thirds water?" (*All right*) These are words that must be said. (*All right*)

Now don't think you have me in a bind today. I'm not talking about communism. What I'm talking about is far beyond communism. (*Yeah*) My inspiration didn't come from Karl Marx (*Speak*); my inspiration didn't come from Engels; my inspiration didn't come from Trotsky; my inspiration didn't come from Lenin. Yes, I read *Communist Manifesto* and *Das Kapital* a long time ago (*Well*), and I saw that maybe Marx didn't follow Hegel enough. (*All right*) He took his dialectics, but he left out his idealism and his spiritualism. And he went over to a German philosopher by the name of Feuerbach, and took his materialism and made it into a system that he called "dialectical materialism." (*Speak*) I have to reject that.

What I'm saying to you this morning is communism forgets that life is individual. (*Yes*) Capitalism forgets that life is social. (*Yes, Go ahead*) And the kingdom of brotherhood is found neither in the thesis of communism nor the antithesis of capitalism, but in a higher synthesis. (*Speak*) [*Applause*] It is found in a higher synthesis (*Come on*) that combines the truths of both. (*Yes*) Now when I say questioning the whole society, it means ultimately coming to see that the problem of racism, the problem of economic exploitation, and the problem of war are all tied together. (*All right*) These are the triple evils that are interrelated.

And if you will let me be a preacher just a little bit. (*Speak*) One day [*Applause*], one night, a juror came to Jesus (*Yes sir*) and he wanted to know what he could do to be saved. (*Yeah*) Jesus didn't get bogged down on the kind of isolated approach of what you shouldn't do. Jesus didn't say, "Now, Nicodemus, you must stop lying." He didn't say, "Nicodemus, now you must not commit adultery." He didn't say, "Now, Nicodemus, you must stop cheating if you are doing that." He didn't say, "Nicodemus, you must stop drinking liquor if you are doing that excessively." He said something altogether different, because Jesus realized something basic (*Yes*): that if a man will lie, he will steal. (*Yes*) And if a man will steal, he will kill. (*Yes*) So instead of just getting bogged down on one thing, Jesus looked at him and said, "Nicodemus, you must be born again." (*Speak*) [*Applause*]

In other words, "Your whole structure (*Yes*) must be changed." [*Applause*] A nation that will keep people in slavery for 244 years will "thingify" them and make them things. (*Speak*) And therefore, they will exploit them and poor people generally economically. (*Yes*) And a nation that will exploit economically will have to have foreign investments and everything else, and it will have to use its military might to protect them. All of these problems are tied together. (*Yes*) [*Applause*]

What I'm saying today is that we must go from this convention and say, "America, you must be born again!" [*Applause*]

And so I conclude by saying today that we have a task, and let us go out with a divine dissatisfaction. (*Yes*)

Let us be dissatisfied until America will no longer have a high blood pressure of creeds and an anemia of deeds. (*All right*)

Let us be dissatisfied (*Yes*) until the tragic walls that separate the outer city of wealth and comfort from the inner city of poverty and despair shall be crushed by the battering rams of the forces of justice.

Let us be dissatisfied (*Yes*) until those who live on the outskirts of hope are brought into the metropolis of daily security.

Let us be dissatisfied (*Yes*) until slums are cast into the junk heaps of history (*Yes*), and every family will live in a decent, sanitary home.

Let us be dissatisfied (*Yes*) until the dark yesterdays of segregated schools will be transformed into bright tomorrows of quality integrated education.

Let us be dissatisfied until integration is not seen as a problem but as an opportunity to participate in the beauty of diversity.

Let us be dissatisfied (*All right*) until men and women, however black they may be, will be judged on the basis of the content of their character, not on the basis of the color of their skin. (*Yeah*) Let us be dissatisfied. [*Applause*]

Let us be dissatisfied (*Well*) until every state capitol (*Yes sir*) will be housed by a governor who will do justly, who will love mercy, and who will walk humbly with his God.

Let us be dissatisfied [*Applause*] until from every

city hall, justice will roll down like waters, and right-eousness like a mighty stream. (*Yes*)

Let us be dissatisfied (*Yes*) until that day when the lion and the lamb shall lie down together (*Yes*), and every man will sit under his own vine and fig tree, and none shall be afraid.

Let us be dissatisfied (*Yes*), until men will recognize that out of one blood (*Yes*) God made all men to dwell upon the face of the earth. (*Speak sir*)

Let us be dissatisfied until that day when nobody will shout, "White Power!" when nobody will shout, "Black Power!" but everybody will talk about God's power and human power. [*Applause*]

And I must confess, my friends (*Yes sir*), that the road ahead will not always be smooth. (*Yes*) There will still be rocky places of frustration (*Yes*) and me-andering points of bewilderment. There will be in-evitable setbacks here and there. (*Yes*) And there will be those moments when the buoyancy of hope will be transformed into the fatigue of despair. (*Well*) Our dreams will sometimes be shattered and our ethereal hopes blasted. (*Yes*) We may again, with tear-drenched eyes, have to stand before the bier of some coura-geous civil rights worker whose life will be snuffed out by the dastardly acts of bloodthirsty mobs. (*Well*) But difficult and painful as it is, we must walk on in the days ahead with an audacious faith in the future. (*Well*) And as we continue our charted course, we may gain consolation from the words so nobly left by that great black bard, who was also a great freedom fighter of yesterday, James Weldon Johnson (*Yes*):

Stony the road we trod (*Yes*),
Bitter the chastening rod
Felt in the days
When hope unborn had died. (*Yes*)

Yet with a steady beat,
Have not our weary feet
Come to the place
For which our fathers sighed?

We have come over a way
That with tears has been watered. (*Well*)
We have come treading our paths
Through the blood of the slaughtered.

Out from the gloomy past,
Till now we stand at last (*Yes*)
Where the bright gleam
Of our bright star is cast.

Let this affirmation be our ringing cry. (*Well*) It will give us the courage to face the uncertainties of the future. It will give our tired feet new strength as we continue our forward stride toward the city of freedom. (*Yes*) When our days become dreary with low-hovering clouds of despair (*Well*), and when our nights become darker than a thousand midnights (*Well*), let us remember that there is a creative force in this universe working to pull down the gigantic mountains of evil (*Well*), a power that is able to make a way out of no way (*Yes*) and transform dark yesterdays into bright tomorrows. (*Speak*)

Let us realize that the arc of the moral universe is long, but it bends toward justice. Let us realize that William Cullen Bryant is right: "Truth, crushed to earth, will rise again." Let us go out realizing that the Bible is right: "Be not deceived. God is not mocked. (*Oh yeah*) Whatsoever a man soweth (*Yes*), that (*Yes*) shall he also reap." This is our hope for the future, and with this faith we will be able to sing in some not too distant tomorrow, with a cosmic past tense: "We have overcome! (*Yes*) We have overcome! Deep in my heart, I *did* believe (*Yes*) we would overcome." [*Applause*]

DELIVERED AT THE ELEVENTH ANNUAL CONVENTION OF THE
SOUTHERN CHRISTIAN LEADERSHIP CONFERENCE,
ATLANTA, GEORGIA,
16 AUGUST 1967.

I'VE BEEN
TO THE
MOUNTAINTOP

INTRODUCTION BY ANDREW YOUNG

No speech of Martin Luther King's has provoked as much discussion and debate as the message he gave to the people of Memphis, Tennessee, at the Bishop Charles Mason Temple Church of God in Christ the night before he was assassinated. He spoke without notes and seemingly without thought as he poured forth a powerful stream-of-consciousness narrative before a standing-room crowd of eleven thousand people. It was awesome, and the response of the people produced what German theologian Dr. Rudolf Otto described in his classic *The Idea of the Holy* as a powerful spiritual transformation of an earthly situation into a transcendent religious moment via the *"mysterium transmondum."* God was in this place.

And yet, none of those close to Martin thought there was anything final about the address. We had heard him make the same references on several previous occasions—usually, I might add, when the situation was in some way dangerous. Nevertheless, we had all lived through these dangers and there was no reason to believe we would not do so again. Memphis did not seem as dangerous as Philadelphia, Mississippi, in 1964 or Chicago in 1967—other times when Martin had reminded us that he had "seen the Promised Land."

Martin Luther King had lived his life in the shadow of the cross for the past decade. As a young author, twenty-nine years old, he had been stabbed with a letter opener by a demented woman in Harlem. He often referred to the fact that the blade pressed against the main aorta of his heart, and if he had merely sneezed, it would have severed the artery and he would have bled to death.

He once received a beautiful note from a ten-year-old who said, "I am a little white girl, but I thank God that you didn't sneeze."

Martin often discussed this near-death experience to remind his followers that death was an ever-present possibility. He usually did so in a rather joking manner, concluding for us that we had better be ready to die. "If you haven't found something for which you're willing to die, you're not fit to live," he said.

On more serious occasions, which were very rare, he reminded us of the scar shaped like a crucifix that remained on his chest as a result of the event. "Each morning as I brush my teeth and wash my face, I am reminded by the cross-shaped scar on my chest that each and any day could be my last day on this earth." Then he'd smile and say we'd better make sure that what we were doing was worth dying for.

April 3, 1968, had been a dreary day. We had come back to Memphis only because Martin wanted us to, since our previous march—which had begun peacefully—had been disrupted by rowdy young people paid to promote a violent confrontation with police. We were accustomed to provocateurs within, and attempts at distortion and misinformation from U.S. government sources, but this was a simple garbage workers' strike. Union recognition and a wage that would at least reach the poverty level were the simple goals of the demonstration. Who could reasonably be threatened by such minimal objectives in this day and age?

We were not aware, however, of how seriously threatened the Congress and the White House were at the thought of three thousand disciplined, organized, nonviolent protesters coming to Washington to wage a campaign for the rights of the poor. After all, President Lyndon Johnson had launched a War on Poverty only to have it bogged down by the Vietnam War. Martin's hope was to free up the Johnson administration to get back to a domestic agenda, for no nation could survive with people isolated on a "lonely island of poverty in the midst of a vast ocean of material prosperity." He also warned that the bombs we dropped on Vietnam would explode at home in inflation and unemployment.

The fears were greater than we imagined. Martin must have felt those fears because he was fighting a cold and fearing the flu, something that only happened when he was feeling enormous stress. He was never sick and seldom took medicine. Physically, he was as strong as a bull. But when the internal demons of doubt and anxiety clawed at him, he would feign illness and go in for a checkup, to rest and give himself time to think. (He was in St. Joseph's Infirmary in Atlanta in 1964 when he received word that he had been awarded the Nobel Prize for Peace.)

On April 3, 1968, he had been feeling ill and talking about taking a few days off for a checkup. He was as depressed as I'd ever known him to be. He decided he was not going to the church and asked Ralph Abernathy to speak and apologize for him. But when Ralph and I arrived and saw the overflow crowd at Mason Temple, we sent Bernard Lee back to the hotel to ask Martin to come and simply make an appearance. Ralph would speak; Martin would simply make a few remarks.

Ralph Abernathy's introduction was more than a half hour long. He reminded Martin and the crowd of the long struggle they'd waged beginning with Montgomery in 1955. It was classic Ralph—country preacher, friend, and brother—whose rousing oratory raised the hopes and spirit of the crowd so much that Martin, who had been physically feverish, forgot himself and reached down into his well of spiritual strength and gave his last prophecy.

Did he know? He always knew some speech would be his last.

Was he afraid? Not on your life!

The next day was one of the happiest of his life. Surrounded by his brother, his staff, and close friends of the movement, he laughed and joked all day until it was time to go to dinner at 6:00 P.M.

As he stood on the balcony waiting for Ralph to get ready and trying to decide whether it was necessary to take a coat, a shot rang out.

He was killed instantly as the bullet severed his spinal cord just below the chin.

Only then did his spirit begin to soar across the oceans and into the hearts of people seeking freedom everywhere.

They killed the dreamer at thirty-nine years of age, but the dream will live on into the new millennium, when men and women must still learn to resolve their problems with the force of truth, the power of love, and faith in the Spirit to lead us all into a new promised land, "where the wicked shall keep from troubling, and the weary shall be at rest."

I'VE BEEN
TO THE
MOUNTAINTOP

Thank you very kindly, my friends. As I listened to Ralph Abernathy and his eloquent and generous introduction and then thought about myself, I wondered who he was talking about. [*Laughter*] It's always good to have your closest friend and associate to say something good about you, and Ralph Abernathy is the best friend that I have in the world.

I'm delighted to see each of you here tonight in spite of a storm warning. You reveal that you are determined [*Audience:*] (*Right*) to go on anyhow. (*Yeah, All right*) Something is happening in Memphis, something is happening in our world. And you know, if I were standing at the beginning of time with the possibility of taking a kind of general and panoramic view of the whole of human history up to now, and the Almighty said to me, "Martin Luther King, which age would you like to live in?" I would take my mental flight by Egypt (*Yeah*), and I would watch God's children in their magnificent trek from the dark dungeons of Egypt through, or rather, across the Red Sea, through the wilderness, on toward the Promised Land.

And in spite of its magnificence, I wouldn't stop there. (*All right*)

I would move on by Greece, and take my mind to Mount Olympus. And I would see Plato, Aristotle, Socrates, Euripides, and Aristophanes assembled around the Parthenon [*Applause*], and I would watch them around the Parthenon as they discussed the great and eternal issues of reality. But I wouldn't stop there. (*Oh yeah*)

I would go on even to the great heyday of the Roman Empire (*Yes*), and I would see developments around there, through various emperors and leaders. But I wouldn't stop there. (*Keep on*)

I would even come up to the day of the Renaissance and get a quick picture of all that the Renaissance did for the cultural and aesthetic life of man. But I wouldn't stop there. (*Yeah*)

I would even go by the way that the man for whom I'm named had his habitat, and I would watch Martin Luther as he tacks his ninety-five theses on the door at the church of Wittenberg. But I wouldn't stop there. (*All right*)

I would come on up even to 1863 and watch a vacillating president by the name of Abraham Lincoln finally come to the conclusion that he had to sign the Emancipation Proclamation. But I wouldn't stop there. (*Yeah*) [*Applause*]

I would even come up to the early thirties and see a man grappling with the problems of the bankruptcy of his nation, and come with an eloquent cry that "we have nothing to fear but fear itself." But I wouldn't stop there. (*All right*)

Strangely enough, I would turn to the Almighty and say, "If you allow me to live just a few years in the second half of the twentieth century, I will be happy." [*Applause*]

Now that's a strange statement to make because the world is all messed up. The nation is sick, trouble is in the land, confusion all around. That's a strange statement. But I know, somehow, that only when it is dark enough can you see the stars. (*All right, Yes*) And I see God working in this period of the twentieth century in a way that men in some strange way are responding. Something is happening in our world. (*Yeah*) The masses of people are rising up. And wherever they are assembled today, whether they are in Johannesburg, South Africa; Nairobi, Kenya; Accra, Ghana; New York City; Atlanta, Georgia; Jackson, Mississippi; or Memphis, Tennessee, the cry is always the same: "We want to be free." [*Applause*]

And another reason that I'm happy to live in this period is that we have been forced to a point where we are going to have to grapple with the problems that men have been trying to grapple with through history, but the demands didn't force them to do it. Survival demands that we grapple with them. (*Yes*) Men for years now have been talking about war and peace. But now no longer can they just talk about it. It is no longer a choice between violence and nonviolence in this world; it's nonviolence or nonexistence. That is where we are today. [*Applause*]

And also, in the human rights revolution, if something isn't done and done in a hurry to bring the colored peoples of the world out of their long years of poverty, their long years of hurt and neglect, the whole world is doomed. (*All right*) [*Applause*] Now I'm just happy that God has allowed me to live in this period, to see what is unfolding. And I'm happy that he's allowed me to be in Memphis. (*Oh yeah*)

I can remember [*Applause*], I can remember when Negroes were just going around, as Ralph has said so often, scratching where they didn't itch and laughing when they were not tickled. [*Laughter, applause*] But that day is all over. (*Yeah*) [*Applause*] We mean business now and we are determined to gain our rightful place in God's world. (*Yeah*) [*Applause*] And that's all this whole thing is about. We aren't engaged in any negative protest and in any negative arguments with anybody. We are saying that we are determined to be men. We are determined to be people. (*Yeah*) We are saying [*Applause*], we are saying that we are God's children. (*Yeah*) [*Applause*] And if we are God's children, we don't have to live like we are forced to live.

Now what does all of this mean in this great period of history? It means that we've got to stay together. (*Yeah*) We've got to stay together and maintain unity. You know, whenever Pharaoh wanted to prolong the period of slavery in Egypt, he had a favorite, favorite formula for doing it. What was that? He kept the slaves fighting among themselves. [*Applause*] But whenever the slaves get together, something happens in Pharaoh's court, and he cannot hold the slaves in slavery. When the slaves get together, that's the beginning of getting out of slavery. [*Applause*] Now let us maintain unity.

Secondly, let us keep the issues where they are.

(*Right*) The issue is injustice. The issue is the refusal of Memphis to be fair and honest in its dealings with its public servants, who happen to be sanitation workers. [*Applause*] Now we've got to keep attention on that. (*That's right*) That's always the problem with a little violence. You know what happened the other day, and the press dealt only with the window breaking. (*That's right*) I read the articles. They very seldom got around to mentioning the fact that 1,300 sanitation workers are on strike, and that Memphis is not being fair to them, and that Mayor Loeb is in dire need of a doctor. They didn't get around to that. (*Yeah*) [*Applause*]

Now we're going to march again, and we've got to march again (*Yeah*), in order to put the issue where it is supposed to be (*Yeah*) [*Applause*] and force everybody to see that there are thirteen hundred of God's children here suffering (*That's right*), sometimes going hungry, going through dark and dreary nights wondering how this thing is going to come out. That's the issue. (*That's right*) And we've got to say to the nation, we know how it's coming out. For when people get caught up with that which is right and they are willing to sacrifice for it, there is no stopping point short of victory. [*Applause*]

We aren't going to let any mace stop us. We are masters in our nonviolent movement in disarming police forces. They don't know what to do. I've seen them so often. I remember in Birmingham, Alabama, when we were in that majestic struggle there, we would move out of the Sixteenth Street Baptist Church day after day. By the hundreds we would move out, and

Bull Connor would tell them to send the dogs forth, and they did come. But we just went before the dogs singing, "Ain't gonna let nobody turn me around." [*Applause*] Bull Connor next would say, "Turn the fire hoses on." (*Yeah*) And as I said to you the other night, Bull Connor didn't know history. He knew a kind of physics that somehow didn't relate to the trans-physics that we knew about. And that was the fact that there was a certain kind of fire that no water could put out. [*Applause*] And we went before the fire hoses. (*Yeah*) We had known water. (*All right*) If we were Baptist or some other denominations, we had been immersed. If we were Methodist and some others, we had been sprinkled. But we knew water. That couldn't stop us. [*Applause*]

And we just went on before the dogs and we would look at them, and we'd go on before the water hoses and we would look at it. And we'd just go on singing, "Over my head, I see freedom in the air." (*Yeah*) [*Applause*] And then we would be thrown into paddy wagons, and sometimes we were stacked in there like sardines in a can. (*All right*) And they would throw us in, and old Bull would say, "Take 'em off." And they did, and we would just go on in the paddy wagon singing, "We Shall Overcome." (*Yeah*) And every now and then we'd get in jail, and we'd see the jailers looking through the windows being moved by our prayers (*Yes*) and being moved by our words and our songs. (*Yes*) And there was a power there which Bull Connor couldn't adjust to (*All right*), and so we ended up transforming Bull into a steer, and we won our struggle in Birmingham. [*Applause*]

Now we've got to go on in Memphis just like that. I call upon you to be with us when we go out Monday. (*Yes*) Now about injunctions. We have an injunction and we're going into court tomorrow morning (*Go ahead*) to fight this illegal, unconstitutional injunction. All we say to America is be true to what you said on paper. [*Applause*] If I lived in China or even Russia, or any totalitarian country, maybe I could understand some of these illegal injunctions. Maybe I could understand the denial of certain basic First Amendment privileges, because they haven't committed themselves to that over there. But somewhere I read of the freedom of assembly. Somewhere I read (*Yes*) of the freedom of speech. (*Yes*) Somewhere I read (*All right*) of the freedom of press. (*Yes*) Somewhere I read (*Yes*) that the greatness of America is the right to protest for right. [*Applause*] And so just as I say we aren't going to let any dogs or water hoses turn us around, we aren't going to let any injunction turn us around. [*Applause*] We are going on. We need all of you.

You know, what's beautiful to me is to see all of these ministers of the Gospel. (*Amen*) It's a marvelous picture. (*Yes*) Who is it that is supposed to articulate the longings and aspirations of the people more than the preacher? Somehow the preacher must have a kind of fire shut up in his bones (*Yes*), and whenever injustice is around he must tell it. (*Yes*) Somehow the preacher must be an Amos, who said, "When God speaks, who can but prophesy?" (*Yes*) Again with Amos, "Let justice roll down like waters and righteousness like a mighty stream." (*Yes*) Somehow the preacher must say with Jesus, "The spirit of the Lord is upon me (*Yes*), because He hath anointed me (*Yes*), and He's anointed me to deal with the problems of the poor." (*Go ahead*)

And I want to commend the preachers, under the leadership of these noble men: James Lawson, one who has been in this struggle for many years. He's been to jail for struggling; he's been kicked out of Vanderbilt University for this struggling; but he's still going on, fighting for the rights of his people. [*Applause*] Reverend Ralph Jackson, Billy Kiles; I could just go right on down the list, but time will not permit. But I want to thank all of them, and I want you to thank them because so often preachers aren't concerned about anything but themselves. [*Applause*] And I'm always happy to see a relevant ministry. It's all right to talk about long white robes over yonder, in all of its symbolism, but ultimately people want some suits and dresses and shoes to wear down here. [*Applause*] It's all right to talk about streets flowing with milk and honey, but God has commanded us to be concerned about the slums down here and His children who can't eat three square meals a day. [*Applause*] It's all right to talk about the new Jerusalem, but one day God's preacher must talk about the new New York, the new Atlanta, the new Philadelphia, the new Los Angeles, the new Memphis, Tennessee. [*Applause*] This is what we have to do.

Now the other thing we'll have to do is this: always anchor our external direct action with the power of economic withdrawal. Now we are poor people, individually we are poor when you compare us with white society in America. We are poor. Never stop and forget that collectively, that means all of us together, collectively we are richer than all the nations in the world, with the exception of nine. Did you ever think about that? After you leave the United States, Soviet Russia, Great Britain, West Germany, France, and I could name the others, the American Negro collectively is richer than most nations of the world. We have an annual income of more than thirty billion dollars a year, which is more than all of the exports of the United States and more than the national budget of Canada. Did you know that? That's power right there, if we know how to pool it. (*Yeah*) [*Applause*]

We don't have to argue with anybody. We don't have to curse and go around acting bad with our words. We don't need any bricks and bottles; we don't need any Molotov cocktails. (*Yes*) We just need to go around to these stores (*Yes sir*), and to these massive industries in our country (*Amen*), and say, "God sent us by here (*All right*) to say to you that you're not treating His children right. (*That's right*) And we've come by here to ask you to make the first item on your agenda fair treatment where God's children are concerned. Now if you are not prepared to do that, we do have an agenda that we must follow. And our agenda calls for withdrawing economic support from you." [*Applause*]

And so, as a result of this, we are asking you tonight (*Amen*) to go out and tell your neighbors not to buy Coca-Cola in Memphis. (*Yeah*) [*Applause*] Go by and tell them not to buy Sealtest milk. (*Yeah*) [*Applause*]

Tell them not to buy—what is the other bread?—
Wonder Bread. [*Applause*] And what is the other
bread company, Jesse? Tell them not to buy Hart's
bread. [*Applause*] As Jesse Jackson has said, up to now
only the garbage men have been feeling pain. Now
we must kind of redistribute the pain. [*Applause*] We
are choosing these companies because they haven't
been fair in their hiring policies, and we are choosing them because they can begin the process of saying they are going to support the needs and the rights
of these men who are on strike. And then they can
move on downtown and tell Mayor Loeb to do what
is right. (*That's right, Speak*) [*Applause*]

Now not only that, we've got to strengthen black
institutions. (*That's right, Yeah*) I call upon you to take
your money out of the banks downtown and deposit
your money in Tri-State Bank. (*Yeah*) [*Applause*] We
want a "bank-in" movement in Memphis. (*Yes*) Go
by the savings and loan association. I'm not asking
you something that we don't do ourselves in SCLC.
Judge Hooks and others will tell you that we have an
account here in the savings and loan association from
the Southern Christian Leadership Conference. We
are telling you to follow what we're doing, put your
money there. [*Applause*] You have six or seven black
insurance companies here in the city of Memphis.
Take out your insurance there. We want to have an
"insurance-in." [*Applause*] Now these are some prac-
tical things that we can do. We begin the process of
building a greater economic base, and at the same
time, we are putting pressure where it really hurts.

(*There you go*) And I ask you to follow through here. [*Applause*]

Now let me say as I move to my conclusion that we've got to give ourselves to this struggle until the end. (*Amen*) Nothing would be more tragic than to stop at this point in Memphis. We've got to see it through. [*Applause*] And when we have our march, you need to be there. If it means leaving work, if it means leaving school, be there. [*Applause*] Be concerned about your brother. You may not be on strike (*Yeah*), but either we go up together or we go down together. [*Applause*] Let us develop a kind of dangerous unselfishness.

One day a man came to Jesus and he wanted to raise some questions about some vital matters of life. At points he wanted to trick Jesus (*That's right*), and show him that he knew a little more than Jesus knew and throw him off base. [*Recording interrupted*] Now that question could have easily ended up in a philosophical and theological debate. But Jesus immediately pulled that question from midair and placed it on a dangerous curve between Jerusalem and Jericho. (*Yeah*) And he talked about a certain man who fell among thieves. (*Sure*) You remember that a Levite (*Sure*) and a priest passed by on the other side; they didn't stop to help him. Finally, a man of another race came by. (*Yes sir*) He got down from his beast, decided not to be compassionate by proxy. But he got down with him, administered first aid, and helped the man in need. Jesus ended up saying this was the good man, this was the great man because he had the capacity to project the "I" into the "thou," and to be concerned about his brother.

Now, you know, we use our imagination a great deal to try to determine why the priest and the Levite didn't stop. At times we say they were busy going to a church meeting, an ecclesiastical gathering, and they had to get on down to Jerusalem so they wouldn't be late for their meeting. (*Yeah*) At other times we would speculate that there was a religious law that one who was engaged in religious ceremonials was not to touch a human body twenty-four hours before the ceremony. (*All right*) And every now and then we begin to wonder whether maybe they were not going down to Jerusalem, or down to Jericho, rather, to organize a Jericho Road Improvement Association. [*Laughter*] That's a possibility. Maybe they felt that it was better to deal with the problem from the causal root, rather than to get bogged down with an individual effect. [*Laughter*]

But I'm going to tell you what my imagination tells me. It's possible that those men were afraid. You see, the Jericho Road is a dangerous road. (*That's right*) I remember when Mrs. King and I were first in Jerusalem. We rented a car and drove from Jerusalem down to Jericho. (*Yeah*) And as soon as we got on that road I said to my wife, "I can see why Jesus used this as the setting for his parable." It's a winding, meandering road. (*Yes*) It's really conducive for ambushing. You start out in Jerusalem, which is about twelve hundred miles, or rather, twelve hundred feet above sea level. And by the time you get down to Jericho fifteen or twenty minutes later, you're about twenty-two hundred feet below sea level. That's a dangerous road. (*Yes*) In the days of Jesus it came to be known as the "Bloody Pass." And you know, it's possible that the priest and the Levite looked over that man on the ground and wondered if the robbers were still around. (*Go ahead*) Or it's possible that they felt that the man on the ground was merely faking (*Yeah*), and he was acting like he had been robbed and hurt in order to seize them over there, lure them there for quick and easy seizure. (*Oh yeah*) And so the first question that the priest asked, the first question that the Levite asked was, "If I stop to help this man, what will happen to me?" (*All right*)

But then the Good Samaritan came by, and he reversed the question: "If I do not stop to help this man, what will happen to him?" That's the question before you tonight. (*Yes*) Not, "If I stop to help the sanitation workers, what will happen to my job?" Not, "If I stop to help the sanitation workers, what will happen to all of the hours that I usually spend in my office every day and every week as a pastor?" (*Yes*) The question is not, "If I stop to help this man in need, what will happen to me?" The question is, "If I do *not* stop to help the sanitation workers, what will happen to them?" That's the question. [*Applause*]

Let us rise up tonight with a greater readiness. Let us stand with a greater determination. And let us move on in these powerful days, these days of challenge, to make America what it ought to be. We have an opportunity to make America a better nation. (*Amen*)

And I want to thank God, once more, for allowing me to be here with you. (*Yes sir*) You know, several years ago I was in New York City autographing the first book that I had written. And while sitting there autographing books, a demented black woman came up. The only question I heard from her was, "Are you Martin Luther King?" And I was looking down writing and I said, "Yes."

The next minute I felt something beating on my chest. Before I knew it I had been stabbed by this demented woman. I was rushed to Harlem Hospital. It was a dark Saturday afternoon. And that blade had gone through, and the X rays revealed that the tip of the blade was on the edge of my aorta, the main artery. And once that's punctured you're drowned in your own blood; that's the end of you. (*Yes sir*) It came out in the *New York Times* the next morning that if I had merely sneezed, I would have died.

Well, about four days later, they allowed me, after the operation, after my chest had been opened and the blade had been taken out, to move around in the wheelchair in the hospital. They allowed me to read some of the mail that came in, and from all over the states and the world kind letters came in. I read a few, but one of them I will never forget. I had received one from the president and the vice president; I've forgotten what those telegrams said. I'd received a visit and a letter from the governor of New York, but I've forgotten what that letter said. (*Yes*)

But there was another letter (*All right*) that came from a little girl, a young girl who was a student at the White Plains High School. And I looked at that letter and I'll never forget it. It said simply, "Dear Dr. King: I am a ninth-grade student at the White Plains

High School." She said, "While it should not matter, I would like to mention that I'm a white girl. I read in the paper of your misfortune and of your suffering. And I read that if you had sneezed, you would have died. And I'm simply writing you to say that I'm so happy that you didn't sneeze." (*Yes*) [*Applause*]

And I want to say tonight [*Applause*], I want to say tonight that I, too, am happy that I didn't sneeze. Because if I had sneezed (*All right*), I wouldn't have been around here in 1960 (*Well*), when students all over the South started sitting-in at lunch counters. And I knew that as they were sitting in, they were really standing up (*Yes sir*) for the best in the American dream and taking the whole nation back to those great wells of democracy, which were dug deep by the founding fathers in the Declaration of Independence and the Constitution.

If I had sneezed (*Yes*), I wouldn't have been around here in 1961, when we decided to take a ride for freedom and ended segregation in interstate travel. (*All right*)

If I had sneezed (*Yes*), I wouldn't have been around here in 1962, when Negroes in Albany, Georgia, decided to straighten their backs up. And whenever men and women straighten their backs up, they are going somewhere, because a man can't ride your back unless it is bent.

If I had sneezed [*Applause*], if I had sneezed, I wouldn't have been here in 1963 (*All right*), when the black people of Birmingham, Alabama, aroused the conscience of this nation and brought into being the Civil Rights Bill.

If I had sneezed, I wouldn't have had a chance later that year, in August, to try to tell America about a dream that I had had. (*Yes*)

If I had sneezed [*Applause*], I wouldn't have been down in Selma, Alabama, to see the great movement there.

If I had sneezed, I wouldn't have been in Memphis to see a community rally around those brothers and sisters who are suffering. (*Yes*) I'm so happy that I didn't sneeze.

And they were telling me. [*Applause*] Now it doesn't matter now. (*Go ahead*) It really doesn't matter what happens now. I left Atlanta this morning, and as we got started on the plane—there were six of us—the pilot said over the public address system: "We are sorry for the delay, but we have Dr. Martin Luther King on the plane. And to be sure that all of the bags were checked, and to be sure that nothing would be wrong on the plane, we had to check out everything carefully. And we've had the plane protected and guarded all night."

And then I got into Memphis. And some began to say the threats, or talk about the threats that were out (*Yeah*), or what would happen to me from some of our sick white brothers.

Well, I don't know what will happen now; we've got some difficult days ahead. (*Amen*) But it really doesn't matter with me now, because I've been to the mountaintop. (*Yeah*) [*Applause*] And I don't mind. [*Applause continues*] Like anybody, I would like to live a long life—longevity has its place. But I'm not concerned about that now. I just want to do God's will.

(*Yeah*) And He's allowed me to go up to the mountain. (*Go ahead*) And I've looked over (*Yes sir*), and I've seen the Promised Land. (*Go ahead*) I may not get there with you. (*Go ahead*) But I want you to know tonight (*Yes*), that we, as a people, will get to the Promised Land. [*Applause*] (*Go ahead, Go ahead*) And so I'm happy tonight; I'm not worried about anything; I'm not fearing any man. Mine eyes have seen the glory of the coming of the Lord. [*Applause*]

DELIVERED AT BISHOP CHARLES MASON TEMPLE,
MEMPHIS, TENNESSEE,
3 APRIL 1968.

Acknowledgments

This collection is a product of the King Papers Project's continuing effort to disseminate information about King's life and ideas. The project's principal mission is to produce The Papers of Martin Luther King, Jr., an authoritative fourteen-volume edition of King's most significant correspondence, sermons, speeches, published writings, and unpublished manuscripts. The Martin Luther King, Jr., Center for Nonviolent Social Change, Inc., initiated this long-term documentary research and publication venture, which is being conducted in association with the King Estate, Stanford University, and the University of California Press. Major financial supporters of the King Papers Project include the National Endowment for the Humanities, the National Historical Publications and Records Commission, the Lilly Endowment, and the Woodside Summit Group.

Assembling and editing King's landmark speeches required the cooperation of many individuals. The editors wish to express special appreciation for the assistance of King Center founder Coretta Scott King in bringing together the introductions to the selections and to Dexter Scott King, who has steadfastly supported the King Project's effort to produce popular works that draw upon The Papers. King Center administrator Tricia Harris and librarian Cynthia Lewis facilitated our efforts to acquire recordings, as did Maja Thomas of Time Warner's AudioBook division. Other Time Warner personnel who contributed to this book included Jody Handley and Bob Castillo.

Staff members of the King Papers Project played essential roles in the preparation of the book manuscript. Although it is intended for general readers rather than scholars, the transcriptions were done to the same exacting standards that are evident in their work on behalf of The Papers. Research Assistant Erin Wood was intensely involved in every stage of the manuscript production, applying her exceptional skill and dedication to the difficult task of producing accurate transcriptions from often fragile and fragmentary recordings. Managing editor Susan Carson supervised the acquisition of the recordings on which this collection is based. Other staff members who played lesser, yet vital, roles in producing this book included assistant editors Adrienne Clay and Kerry Taylor; research assistants Tenisha Armstrong and Lauren Araiza; project administrator Jane Abbott; office assistant Regina Convington; and assistant to the director Vicki Brooks. Finally, we also thank the student researchers in our Summer 2000 King Research Program, including Misha Charles, Elizabeth Crocker, Adrienne Denson, Joshua Dougherty, Reygan Harmon, Kris Hoeppner, and Jen Sahrle.